HEALING ARTS PUBLISHING
A DIVISION OF *THE WORLDWIDE CENTER*
EVERGREEN, COLORADO

HEALING THROUGH LOVE

by Marilyn Innerfeld

OTHER HEALING ARTS PUBLISHING BOOKS

The Simple Truth About God — by Christine Lenick

The above titles are available at your local bookstore.
Copies may also be ordered at *The Worldwide Center* website
www.expandedliving.net or by calling
303-674-7704.

The author of this book does not dispense medical
advice or prescribe the use of any technique as a form of
treatment for physical or medical problems without the
advice of a physician, either directly or indirectly. The
intent of the author is only to offer information of a
general nature to help you in your quest for emotional
and spiritual well-being. In the event you use any of
the information in this book for yourself, which is your
constitutional right, the author and the publisher assume
no responsibility for your actions.

Healing Arts Publishing
The Worldwide Center for the Healing Arts, LLC
P.O. Box 4223
Evergreen, CO 80437

Visit our website at www.expandedliving.net

Printed in the United States of America.

ISBN: 0-9711522-1-7
Library of Congress No. 2003103380

Cover and Interior Design by
Michele Renée Ledoux
michele@mledoux.com | www.mledoux.com

This book is available at quantity discounts for bulk
purchases. For information, call 303-674-7704.

DEDICATION

This book is dedicated to...

...my daughters, Jodi and Dara, who chose me to nurture them in this glorious lifetime, and who have nurtured me in return, with unconditional love and acceptance each step of our intertwined paths. You, my girls, are angels walking this earth.

...Hank, who has been my teacher in this lifetime and many lifetimes past. Thank you for your patience, your faith and your vision. I experienced great joy sharing my life and love with so magnificent a Being, and fully honor our mutual choice to explore our new-found freedom.

...my parents and my sister, who have chosen these life experiences with each other and with me, enabling each of us the greatest opportunity to discover the magnificence of who we each are.

...my dear friends Sharon Campbell, Diane Kenny, Colleen Matheson and Nancy Mueller, who have supported me, challenged me and loved me throughout this process.

...Mary Jean, Madlyn, Gennifer and Tweedie, and to the large number of friends and clients who have honored me by embracing their power, thus creating changes in all our lives. You have been my greatest Teachers.

...my soul sister, Christine Lenick, a powerful healer who has honored me with her friendship and love. Together, we share this lifetime with absolute acceptance and knowing of the greatest Truth of all—that we are God. This wondrous Being is my teacher, my partner-in-healing and my most special friend. Thank you, Chris, for your vision of who we truly are...for, in this love, I have found the courage to be all that I am.

Finally, I dedicate this book to you, the Reader, for giving permission to allow change to enter your life. May you know that you are truly magnificent...and perfect. You are here on a glorious adventure. Choose to experience it in total wellness and know that it is yours to create...through love!

Contents

FOREWORD

I created cancer in my life. I didn't know I was creating it, but as I look back on how I was living, I now recognize how I created this experience. It was extraordinary...and challenging. It was frightening, at times overwhelming. But I chose to acknowledge my hand in its creation, and I chose to use all the power I possessed to do what needed to be done to heal.

It took a full year to heal my body of cancer, but it took forty-eight years to create it. Compared to the time it took to create the blocks and the pain within my body and heart, I consider one year a moment of time, but it was a year of wakefulness, in contrast to the time I had spent "asleep" to my choices and personal issues.

This book offers you the opportunity to "wake up." From this moment forth, you can choose to look at your life in all moments, and recognize that you have the power to live as you want to live. It took me forty-eight years to learn this.

You don't know me, although I am no different from you. It doesn't matter how we look, or our religious affiliations, or our choices of behavior. We are all the same—human beings living a physical existence, experiencing moments of joy, moments of sadness, moments of peace, moments of pain, moments of illness. Once we recognize that there is no difference between one human being and another, then we can learn from one another, for our lives always run parallel to the lives of all.

Within these pages I offer you my life story as an example of how we create illness—and how we can heal from illness. It is always a matter of choice.

Nothing occurs in our lives by accident. We can learn to recognize that each moment offers us great opportunity for learning, as well as the opportunity to make new choices and bring about a change based upon the experience of that moment.

I am a medical intuitive. This means that I have the ability to scan a person's body and sense the blocks within. I can see organ systems and feel the blood flow. I know the body's nutritional needs and imbalances. I feel the aches and pains of another person's joints and muscles. Through my work, I choose not only to identify the anomalies, but also to assist the person towards self-healing. I use energy to "jump-start" the healing process, but I hold the person responsible for choosing to heal. I know in my heart that healing can occur when the person makes the choice to heal and acts upon that choice. We each can do anything we choose to do, once we believe in ourSelves.

I have fallen in love with me. I didn't know how wonderful I was until I almost lost my life to cancer. And by choosing selfLove, rather than self-hate, I have healed my heart—and my body—of cancer.

With these words, I am opening my life and my heart to you. In doing so, my intent is to touch your heart as well. Once we choose to accept the oneness of our connection, our hearts and the hearts of all can begin to resonate with acceptance and understanding of who we are.

CHAPTER ONE

Illness as My Greatest Teacher

*I was constantly focusing on healing my physical body, never recognizing
that I needed to heal my heart.*

Many of us strive to fill our lives with joy, love and peace. During the
fifteen years before my illness, this had been a powerful focus for me, as I
experienced the expansion of my spiritual awareness. Like many others,
however, I considered mySelf a failure whenever I had days, or even moments,
of anger, disappointment or other "negative" emotions. After all, should we
not, when seeking inner peace and selfLove, always flow in harmony and
perfection?

Perfection is a word that brings to mind all that we are truly seeking—
joy, serenity, bliss. We see perfection in our lives when things go "right," and
when the opposite occurs and we have a "bad" day or something turns out
"wrong," we believe that the perfection of the moment has been lost, and that
we need once again to strive to recreate harmony.

The truth is simply that *all* moments are perfect, because, regardless
of the experience, we are Beings *choosing* how we will learn. In fact,
through moments of challenge, as well as through moments of joy, we call
forth wonderful opportunities to learn. While living through challenging
moments is rarely fun and can create emotional distress and trauma, we
have *chosen* that reaction to our experience. We can freely and easily choose
different reactions. We can simply learn how to let go of the judgment we

1

make about the circumstances of our lives and ask, in all moments, "What am I supposed to learn from this experience?" By doing this, we allow the experience to simply be an experience. We learn to view all aspects of life and living as *neutral*, thereby liberating ourselves from judgment.

What I am about to share with you is my personal story of illness. I chose it unwittingly, yet it was my personal path to learning about selfLove in the most powerful sense. That I *chose* illness is not something easy to admit, for who in his or her right mind would make such a choice? To choose *cancer* (the word alone fills one with dread) is a powerful opportunity to learn, through a pathway of exploration to one's very core, about life...and love...and death.

Having made this choice in my own life, I had the opportunity to discover my personal magnificence, a discovery I might not have made without the experience. And so, I am grateful for the cancer...and for my choice to heal and live fully in the joy of my life as I live it now.

⊰⊱⊰⊱

In my work as a healing practitioner and medical intuitive, I am able to sense discordant energy within the physical and energetic bodies of clients. Through my knowing, I am also able to assist in the release of the discord, bringing forth healing on many levels, and then guide the client through the completion of their own powerful self-healing. It is a joyous experience for me. I have learned not to judge what I see within the physical and energetic bodies of my clients, but rather to recognize that all aspects of one's Being are in a state of perfection. Whether a client comes to me in the advanced stages of cancer or with a simpler complaint of headaches, my work is always the same—allowing the experience to simply be the experience, without judgment or fear.

I recognize and teach that, to fully heal, it is the heart, representing our experience of selfLove, that must heal. All illness begins with emotional pain created by choices of limitation, and as the pain is released, the physical manifestation of this pain is also released.

Why, then, did I not see mySelf from this same perspective?

In the fall of 1998, I began to bleed lightly from my rectum. This is never a pleasant occurrence, and my heart reacted with a fear I had never felt before. Being a medical intuitive, I chose to self-diagnose and concluded that I was suffering from hemorrhoids. Interestingly, I also chose to keep this information private and did not share it with my close family or friends. I did not want to be reminded that my father, who died of colon cancer, also experienced these same symptoms, and I kept pushing the nagging fear that was growing in my heart away from my mind.

Time passed, and my life and work continued with relative ease. The bleeding was sporadic and I gave it little thought. I had a belief that whatever we focus on grows, and so I chose to "erase" the experience from my thoughts. Can we really do this? We think we can, but there is always a *knowing* that exists, whether or not we acknowledge it. And for me, this *knowing* was growing stronger as time passed.

I was living a dual life: practicing my healing work and powerfully affecting the lives of others in a positive way, but diminishing mySelf by neglecting my own physical needs because of deep-seated fears. I was ignoring the unsettled emotions of my heart, allowing the discordant energies to permeate my physical body more powerfully.

Oddly enough, although I was blessed to be working closely and intimately with my husband Hank and my friend Christine Lenick, both powerful healers and intuitives, it took a while before I mentioned my physical situation to them. The bleeding was getting more intense, and I had a core awareness of something more serious going on, but I was still not ready to face it.

Once I'd shared my concerns with them and other healer friends, Chris confronted me, pointing out that the medical path would be the "most expedient" for my healing. I still interpreted this as an opportunity to heal mySelf energetically and continued to delay consulting a doctor. As an "alternative healer," I was hesitant to follow the medical pathway.

As my symptoms continued, I finally bowed to the pressure of loving family and friends and made an appointment. In my heart, I had decided that I had hemorrhoids, so I convinced mySelf that this was what would be discovered, and that all would be well.

The exam, not wholly pleasant but not as uncomfortable as I had imagined, was brief. A young doctor saw the inner hemorrhoids, agreed with my diagnosis and sent me home with a prescription for the ointments that would bring me the physical healing I desired.

What a relief! And what a powerful sense of joy at the realization that I truly knew my body well enough to heal mySelf—not only in that moment but in all future moments. Doctors would no longer be needed in my life!

I believed fully, and with what seemed to me good reasons, that Western medicine was filled with limitation and diagnosis by-the-book. I also believed that the human touch had been lost in this arena, and that people were treated as bodies without souls, emotional needs or psychological support. I saw doctors as people with large egos and larger pocketbooks, and I did not step back enough to know that the issues were my own.

I viewed alternative healers like mySelf as people dedicated to helping others, who were willing to go into non-scientific realms, delving into areas of the heart and soul to discover the true sources of dis-ease. Without realizing it, I was as judgmental and critical of Western medical practices and models as many traditional medical practitioners are of non-traditional health practitioners.

More importantly, I was unaware that my actions—or inactions—were the reflection of my personal lack of selfLove. While I was challenging mySelf to be my own healer, I was diminishing mySelf in my own eyes...and feeling a sense of failure because I could not seem to heal my bleeding. This sense of failure kept growing as the weeks and months continued.

⇥⟩⟨⇤

Time quickly passed, and while my life was filled with work, growth and change, I experienced continued rectal bleeding. I changed my diet and became a vegetarian, which served to lighten the situation and improve my digestion. I gave up sugar and had given up caffeine and alcohol long before. I increased my nutritional supplements and stayed strong. And I began to slowly lose weight, which brought me joy because I believed, at some level, that the weight loss was due to my dietary changes.

But the bleeding continued.

Since I had recently moved from the East Coast to Colorado, my hair and skin were changing because of the lack of humidity in the air. I was having a difficult time finding a hairdresser who was able to give me a haircut I liked, since I was accustomed to natural curls and an easy hairdo. I heard mySelf complaining to my reflection each morning in the mirror, until, one day, I suddenly had a powerful *knowing* that I might not always be so fortunate as to have such a full and lovely head of hair! It was a stirring deep within me, saying that, if I needed chemotherapy, I could lose all my hair!

So, from that moment forth, I chose to consciously appreciate my hair and all other aspects of mySelf, in an effort to create from love and appreciation, rather than from fear. What I did not want to face was that I had

What do you say to yourself when you look in the mirror?

List the first three things that come to mind. Imagine how powerful your words are—how do these thoughts affect your life?

5

finally become aware of the cancer that was growing in my body...and months passed, with my secret held deep within my heart.

It is not easy keeping so powerful a secret, especially when surrounded by family and friends as loving as mine. What I did not want to face was that I was not loving mySelf enough to ask for assistance, and that my fears, based upon the history of my father's illness and death, were stronger than I even recognized. *I was constantly focusing on healing my physical body, never recognizing that I needed to heal my heart.* What I had yet to learn was that, had my heart been filled with love for Self, the physical and energetic aspects of my healing would have been made possible.

During this time, Chris Lenick and I decided to become business partners and created The Worldwide Center, which is based in Evergreen, Colorado. Life was hectic, and the desire to move into the peace and beauty of the mountains became a priority.

My daughters, now young women, were preparing to leave home, and Hank's own healing practice was expanding, with him beginning to travel more frequently across the country, giving seminars and classes. I chose to continue to ignore my physical body and did not allow mySelf to focus on the weakness growing within me.

But it was only natural for me to feel the effects of the increasing blood loss, and the time came when I could no longer ignore the weight loss and extreme fatigue I was experiencing. I again turned to Chris and asked her to "examine" me as she would another client. We had created a powerful friendship and trust in one another, and I knew that her love for me would give me the information I needed to hear.

Ironically, I was right...but not in the way I expected. As Chris scanned my body, she "saw" a block in my intestinal tract and had the *knowing* that I would strongly benefit from an immediate visit to the doctor, but she also said that I would know in one week's time whether my body would heal itself, or if I needed to care for it medically.

I was happy with this information, which I interpreted as supporting my desire to heal mySelf without going to a doctor for assistance. I still was tied to my beliefs and judgments regarding Western medicine, and focused solely upon the physical, rather than allowing mySelf to see my innermost truth—that my heart needed healing, along with my body.

My fear of loss of personal power through a creation of illness paralyzed me, preventing me from making the more honoring choice of seeking medical support, and my sense of personal failure at my inability to heal mySelf became an issue that my ego could not face. Was I a fraud—able to "heal" others but not mySelf? This experience was challenging the very core of who I was, as well as the joy I experience in my work.

In that moment of experience, I could not see that my choice was based on fear, rather than on selfLove. I did not recognize that I was diminishing mySelf by challenging mySelf to heal without assistance. I worried about what others would think about my inability to heal mySelf. I did not ask mySelf what I was to learn from the experience, and therefore I did not realize that, although I was choosing to heal, my choice to live in judgment, fear and secrecy could have led me to learn what I needed to learn through the experience of death.

We learn in all aspects of life and living. Even in death and continued existence, learning is ongoing. Learning is experienced in all realms of Being. Was I, due to my fear and stubbornness, going to learn my lessons in another lifetime? From the neutrality of all that is, this was a distinct possibility, but one I was blinded by self-judgment from seeing.

Hank and I purchased a beautiful mountain home, and life was filled with the activities surrounding the move. I found mySelf unable to participate fully in the physical aspects of packing, but blamed it on issues other than my health. We are amazing at tricking ourSelves when fear is the motivation! So, life was exciting and hectic and, for me, a bit challenging, but we lived fully in the moment, remaining blissfully unaware of what was to come.

❀❀❀

It was Mother's Day of 2000 when I knew I had lost control. The day was filled with plans, which included visiting my mother-in-law and going out to my favorite restaurant. I was silently struggling to get ready when I knew that I would not be able to leave my home that day. The bleeding was profuse and I was suffering from acute diarrhea.

I sent my family on without me, much to their dismay, and spent the day struggling with both the physical manifestation of my condition and the emotional awareness of my creation. First thing on Monday, I made an emergency appointment for a colonoscopy, which was scheduled for Wednesday afternoon. And I had no choice but to wait.

A colonoscopy is a procedure that enables a doctor to examine the bowels and intestines by using a camera on the end of a long tube, which allows it to travel through the rectum and up the digestive tract. A mild sedative is given to relax the patient, and the procedure takes only about twenty minutes.

Since I had not had any medications in my system for years, the mild sedatives completely knocked me out. I was awakened over an hour later by the doctor speaking loudly and close to my face, repeating over and over, "Marilyn, wake up. You have cancer!"

Although it appeared to him that I was still asleep, I heard him through the haze and thought I kept repeating in response, "Yes, I know. So what?" Later on, I was told I never spoke those words, but they are a distinct and powerful memory.

Yes...I *knew* I had cancer. I had known it for quite some time. I was in denial; I was in fear; I had chosen not to take the actions that would have healed my body sooner, because of my personal judgment of traditional medicine, and my belief that to be a "healer" meant that I had to be able to heal mySelf without help. After all, I was a healing practitioner, a medical intuitive, a psychic. But I remained blinded by my focus on the physical, when the healing needed to be a healing of my heart.

The surgery was scheduled for seven o'clock the following morning. Unable to research and seek our choice of surgeon, we were assigned the doctor who was to perform the surgery. Fortunately, the finest surgeon in the hospital had an unexpected opening in his schedule.

At the mercy of hospital care, I had no choice but to simply allow what was about to transpire. Still under the influence of the drugs and sedatives, I had no opportunity to think...to even care. But I cannot deny the underlying fear that permeated me while I lay in a hospital bed, rather than in the comfort of my home, surrounded by the sights and sounds and smells of the hospital—the lights, the interrupted sleep, the constant ministrations of the nurses.

What was I supposed to learn through this experience? What did I need to release in order to heal fully and completely? Why was this pathway presented to me...and where would it take me?

The next morning, I awoke in time to share the love of my family and friends, and the surgery went as scheduled.

Details are truly unnecessary, except that, when I finally was able to move through the haze of the anesthesia, I took charge of my healing once again. I insisted on having the catheter removed as soon as possible, knowing that going to the bathroom on my own, as physically painful as it was, would increase my healing. I chose to use the morphine drip to its absolute minimum, knowing that morphine and other similar medications keep the body sluggish. I had the nurses remove the tube from my nose and limit the glucose drip as soon as possible, knowing that the sooner I allowed my body to accept food, the sooner its internal workings would revive. I was out of the hospital four days after the day of the operation; the doctors told me their patients generally stay from five to seven days, if not longer.

It was not a battle of wills. It was not stubbornness or ego. It was my *knowing* that I could heal as quickly as I chose to, and that I would heal better and faster at home, where I could eat the foods and take the nutritional supplements that honored me.

Once again, I powerfully took charge of my destiny.

I cannot write this story without admitting that I struggled with fears—fears of having "created" cancer, fears of continued illness, fears of failure. I was not afraid of dying, but I was afraid of how my dying would affect those who loved me.

So, my healing was more than physical. It included going within, into the deepest aspects of Self, and listening to my quietest, innermost voice, which was teaching me why and how and what I was to learn from all of this.

I wanted to free my heart of its pain and release the fears at my core. It took hours of talking, crying, meditating, until I was finally willing to go to the depths of my Being and accept my personal magnificence. This was a bumpy road, for I had to release all judgment of Self and fully accept that I am magnificent. I learned to celebrate mySelf for creating the illness itself, since it had allowed me to finally know my greatest Truth—that I can choose to love mySelf unconditionally.

Importantly, I also learned to honor the modern medical miracles that exist in our technological age: the gifted hands of a surgeon who loves his work and heals the physical body so powerfully; the machines and tests that bring up the numbers and statistics we may not always want to hear, but should know, in order to make powerful and intelligent choices; the drugs that help control and reduce pain, and allow us to be blissfully unaware that our bodies are being cut open, plus the drugs that assist in healing those same incisions. I am deeply grateful for the dedication of the personnel in our modern hospitals, who assist us with tasks that seem so simple when we are healthy—tasks such as bathing, or eating, or simply taking a walk.

And I learned that all forms of healing are equal and available, allowing us to heal the body while we heal our hearts, once we have chosen to allow total healing to take place in our bodies, minds and spirits.

During this illness, I discovered *me*. I discovered my strengths and honored my weaknesses. I allowed mySelf the experience of pain, and I lived through it, whole and perfect.

I recognize that, without this experience, my life would have continued as it was. And, as wonderful as it was, the joys I experience now are sweeter and more appreciated. Illness has been my greatest teacher, for during this journey into wellness, I began to uncover my heart.

CHAPTER TWO

Life After Illness, Life After Trauma

If you always do what you've always done, you'll always get what you've always gotten.

So how does one live after great illness, or great trauma, has touched our lives? I thought I knew the answer to this question, for, as I allowed my body to heal from the surgery that removed the tumor, I continued on with my life. I even thought that I was living differently. But my body still had a message to share—that I had *not* healed my heart!

Less than three months after my surgery, I was scheduled to have a follow-up colonoscopy. I was calmer this time around, and although a lingering fear of illness was shadowing my heart—and my life—I was feeling physically stronger and well. I was feeling better than ever and was back working, living, even playing tennis! However, what ultimately transpired was even more challenging than all that I had experienced before.

My cancer had returned. Through the haze of the moment, I was brought to understand that the cancer had returned at the exact location of the original surgery, indicating that some cells had been missed and were now beginning to grow again.

Imagine the shock of this new information, the feeling of betrayal by my body and my very essence of Being! Imagine the pain, for I knew what I was facing—more surgery and the more definite choice of chemotherapy, with no guarantees.

Prior to that fateful visit with my surgeon, I knew that my body would be changed drastically by this new set of circumstances. I knew, because of my father's illness years before, that, if I wanted to save my body, I would have to lose a large part of my colon.

I will always remember the moment when my doctor tried to give me this piece of news. Before he could tell me, I told him first. "I need a colostomy." I said it simply and peacefully. I had bigger fish to fry. I had my life to save, and I was not going to let the loss of a body part stop me from living.

He was relieved that I understood and grateful that I was able to face the truth that not only would my body change, but so would my life. For me, it was time to rediscover who I was and to allow mySelf the power to reclaim the me that I am.

And so I began to fight.

This surgery, so soon after the first, was much more difficult. I still chose to heal as quickly as possible, but the pain was great and I was frustrated and frightened. However, I was able to return home within days, more quickly than most patients who have had the same surgical procedure. And I also was sent home without a large piece of my colon and with a scary-looking contraption attached to my body that challenged every thought I'd ever had about my physical appearance.

In fact, I had never acknowledged my physical perfection before the surgery; now, in loving mySelf, I was to open my eyes.

Not only was it time to heal my body, it was time to heal my heart. After my first surgery, I had purposefully made choices to change. But although it appeared that the surface of my life had changed, old patterns of self-doubt, diminishment and fear had not. Once I was truly honest with mySelf, I recognized that, within weeks of that first cancer experience, I was back re-living what had always been—inner turmoil, conflict, judgment and pain. And so I spent months remembering, reliving and releasing choices I had made throughout my life. I cried and I laughed; I talked and I meditated. I worked hard and chose foods and nutritional supplements that brought me strength, and had great trust that all would be well. I was surrounded by people who loved me unconditionally and chose to pull away from those who did not. I made choices based on my love for *me*, and I was able to free mySelf of ties that bind.

And I chose to have chemotherapy.

The first time I faced cancer and surgery, I had not believed that I was going to choose to undergo chemotherapy, since there were no indications of any residual cancer in my body. Like many, I had fears about filling my body with the toxic chemicals of chemotherapeutic drugs. The second surgery offered me the same choice, for, once again, I was cancer-free following my surgery. This time, however, the fear of a recurrence was great, and so I made a different choice.

I had once told mySelf that if I ever had cancer, I would *never* choose chemotherapy as my pathway to healing. What a powerful statement that was! And it was based in great fear—fear of feeling sick all the time, of losing my hair, of the toxicity to my body. So many people feel the same way and share their beliefs about the horrors of chemotherapy. Such powerful *judgment* many of us share!

It is important to recognize that *all* healing pathways are equal, simply offering a choice to bring us to health and wellness. We should always, not only when faced with a life or death choice, honor all that is available to us, in order to allow the perfect pathway to unfold.

This was a powerful and difficult decision for me, but one I made with a strong desire to ensure that my body was fully healed of the cancer. I chose to forego the radiation treatments which were recommended, simply in my freedom of choice and the knowing I honored within my heart that they would not benefit me, but accepted the chemotherapy as a preventive measure.

Throughout this experience, Hank and I did not have health insurance. In addition to the medical bills from my two surgeries, facing months of chemotherapy was a daunting undertaking, financially, emotionally and physically. But once I accepted that this was to be my pathway of healing, I was determined to let nothing stand in my way. With family and friends, I researched and interviewed oncologists in the Denver area and chose a doctor who was highly regarded by fellow doctors and patients alike.

When we interviewed him, what drew me to this man was his ability to recognize me as healthy, not sick. For that is what I was. I was allowing chemotherapy to assist me as a preventive pathway to maintaining health, rather than one needed to save my life. And although he strongly suggested that I undergo radiation therapy along with the chemo treatments, he accepted my choice to be treated only with the chemotherapy. I felt deep within my heart that the radiation was unnecessary, and he honored this decision. Had my cancer been a new growth, I might have chosen otherwise.

As I chose to work with this doctor, I shared with him that we had no insurance. He looked deeply into my eyes and told me that I would be given a reasonable payment plan, that his office would assist us in getting medical coverage (which we now have), and that he would never turn away a person who had found him as I had.

How many people fall between the cracks of the health care system because they do not recognize that not having insurance or the money to pay for the best medical care should not limit them to less than the best? Why do we allow our feelings of unworthiness to deter us from getting the best we can? Why do we not love ourSelves so fully that nothing will stand in our way when it comes to taking charge of our healing process? Aren't we always worthy of the best that there is?

I look back on the months of weekly chemo treatments as though they were a dream. It was challenging emotionally and physically, and it brought me to tears of frustration time and time again. I spent a lot of time talking to my body, loving it, loving *me!* I kept asking my body to heal, and I believed that it would listen. I kept asking mySelf what was it that I needed to learn from this experience and I made time to listen. I acknowledged my fear, my pain and my self-recrimination and I chose to release these emotions as they passed through me.

I was fortunate to have retained my hair and my health, dealing with mild nausea and diarrhea, but nothing more unpleasant. I was surrounded, week after week while undergoing the chemotherapy treatments, by people who were wracked with nausea and other side effects. I watched others who had cancer like my own grow grayer and thinner and weaker as the sessions continued, while I maintained my strength, assisted by my own inner healing and nutritional choices. I learned to walk the talk, to the depths of my Being, and love mySelf fully in all ways.

I released the cancer in my heart—my own self-hatred—so that I could allow mySelf to experience acceptance of Self and selfLove. My body has changed, and I look at mySelf in a new way, as though I have different eyes, for through this experience, I recognize the choice to honor all that I am and to appreciate all that I have. I see my body as perfect and focus less and less attention on my "difference" each and every day.

...and I love me! I live more fully, I laugh more freely and I love more openly. I am willing to share all that I am with whoever asks, for, through my experience, perhaps another can learn. As I love mySelf, I love everyone. And I have found the freedom to be *me* in all moments!

⊰⊱⊰⊱

I lived the path of an *alternative* healer for a number of years. Now I choose the path of a *complementary* healer. I have learned that, when a person calls forth illness to his or her life, there can be no stone left unturned to create health once again, so that life and learning can continue, if one chooses. To choose one in judgment of the other simply ignores the benefits of the one not explored, perhaps blocking the healing so desperately sought. Modern medicine can heal the physical body, but this places full emphasis on the body and ignores the heart, where the pain is held within and the creation of illness begins. To maintain physical health, the mind and the spirit must be healed as well.

I have also learned that everything that exists is *neutral.* What this means is that there is no good and no bad, no right and no wrong, no mistakes and no dishonorable choices. What this means is that there are no accidents or illnesses to be viewed in judgment.

We tend to judge ourSelves and our experiences so harshly! We rarely stop to examine the experience in order to learn the lesson being presented. For example, when we are faced with the sudden loss of a job, we experience fear and seldom recognize the moment as a great opportunity to find employment in a field which can create great personal joy! When experiencing a divorce, we focus on the pain, the financial implications, the complications, when, instead, we can choose to recognize the freedom and the opportunity for greater peace of heart. When we create illness, we focus on the illness itself, rather than recognizing the opportunity of looking at our prior choices in life and allowing ourSelves to learn and change.

The most challenging learning I experienced was the realization that I had allowed illness to be my greatest teacher due to self-judgment and even self-hatred. I had diminished mySelf by judging my ability to "heal" my body without assistance as a success or failure. I had focused my choices and my life so narrowly, in fear and judgment, thereby choosing to momentarily forget the truth that everything exists with great purpose, and that we have created all that exists. This includes the modern technologies of our day.

I did not love mySelf for creating the many healing pathways that were always before me. I thought I was where I had yet to go. The healing before me was more than physical, for I needed to acknowledge—and live—my magnificence in *all* ways, even my choice to heal with the assistance of others.

Each of us is wholly and totally magnificent. We create opportunities to learn of this magnificence in many ways and, for me, it was through my body.

We learn differently—sometimes through trauma, and sometimes through joy—but learning occurs in all moments. All learning is equal and each path to learning is as powerful as any other.

My life, from childhood forward, had been filled with pain, judgment, anger and diminishing thoughts and actions. I do not know how or why I made the choice to live this way, but I had. I truly believed I was happy—in my marriage, as a mother, with my chosen professions. I did not choose to acknowledge how my heart was truly experiencing my life—in pain and judgment. Was I good enough as a mother, wife, daughter, friend? Was I caring enough? Was everyone around me happy? (After all, wasn't I responsible for everyone's happiness?) Was I too heavy, spending too much, working hard enough, eating healthy enough, and on and on and on...

...and so I created illness. I called forth cancer in my life to be a great teacher. This illness could have devastated me, paralyzed me from forward movement into greater learning and living. Instead, I allowed this illness to teach me, and I chose to accept the lessons without judging them.

Illness is neutral. Illness is not "bad," although the experience does bring about great challenge. I have come to understand that these challenges enable us to release paradigms of belief which hold us in a more limited or pain-filled experience of Self. Whether we experience illness, accidents, job losses, divorce or trauma, we often also experience emotions and fears and concerns. However, we can also allow the experience to bring us new understanding...and growth...and living...and, ultimately, greater joy.

I called forth illness as my greatest teacher. I know that I have learned and continue to learn great lessons from this experience. Whether it takes a moment or a lifetime, as long as we learn, we embrace change. I began to live my life differently, and I wanted to learn all future lessons through joy. But I acknowledged that my lessons and experiences are always what best serves me, so I no longer judge mySelf or my life, always knowing that *all* life is wondrous!

❧❦❧

So I come to you now as all that I am. I was once quite shy and private, but I have made the choice to share my experience, so that you may perhaps choose to look upon your own choices and bring yourSelf to your own experience of healing, peace, joy and selfLove.

And once again I ask you: How does one live after great illness, or great trauma, has touched our lives?

From my own experience, as well as the experience of many clients with whom I have worked, I have discovered an important truth: *If you always do what you've always done, you'll always get what you've always gotten.*

I had heard these words before, but never recognized their import until it was time to face my own healing. Following my first surgery, I resumed my life almost exactly as it was before. This meant I ate the same, exercised minimally, maintained relationships as they had been, and made choices in my life nearly identical to choices I had made in the past. Thoughts about mySelf and others had not changed; nor had the emotions of pain and self-diminishment deep at my core.

After the second surgery, I finally recognized the importance of accepting responsibility for everything I experience. I also recognized that *it is never about the other.* My life was always the result of *my* choices. And I had never lived. I just dreamt of what living freely would be like.

But it was time to make some changes in my life, because I was choosing to live...and be free!

❧❦❧

Prior to my own personal experience with illness, I had worked with a wonderful and vibrant client who chose to hold onto the life she lived, even though it filled her heart with pain.

Marisa* came to me after being diagnosed with lung cancer. She was filled with fear and was facing long bouts of chemotherapy. I met Marisa during one of my trips across the country and found her to be a very attractive, middle-aged woman, who was meticulous about her appearance and financially comfortable. Marisa had an interesting life and was married to a husband who had been quite promiscuous within their marriage. During our session, she admitted that in order to "get him back," she, too, had allowed herSelf to explore many occasions of infidelity. She had also battled alcoholism for many years. Her appearance belied her pain, and she lived a life filled with secrets deep in her heart. She was, in fact, drowning in the lies and in her attempts to hide her truth from the world.

Working with Marisa was ongoing and challenging. She was willing to share her stories with me, but, try as I might, I could not get her to face her husband and allow herSelf the freedom she needed to clear the energies of pain, guilt and grief that she carried so powerfully. I was equally unable to convince her to change her diet, which consisted of many processed meats and a couple of beers each afternoon or evening to "relax."

What ultimately happened was that Marisa did indeed cure her body of cancer, much to her joy and the joy of her family. However, she once again began to live her life in her old patterns, and she even returned to living them more powerfully, because she was overwhelmed with what it meant to "be alive!"

I often find, when working with clients who "survive" illness, that they are more focused in their choices when facing death; when the specter of death is removed, it is as though they are "lost" and forget how to live their new choices.

The cancer returned. Even during this second bout, Marisa would not change her habits, even those involving food and drink choices. This second cancer was much more tenacious, and Marisa ultimately died.

I use this as an example of how people choose to hold on to old patterns, even following illness or trauma, rather than making the changes which

*All names have been changed to honor the privacy of the clients.

21

would lead them along a pathway of improved health and healing.

Each moment of our lives, we are faced with choices. We can choose to follow patterns we have always followed, or we can choose a different life by exploring new patterns and pathways. Life is filled with experiences, and all experiences are to be honored, for we have brought them forth. If you wish to change an aspect of your life for any reason, know that you have the power in all moments to choose to live differently than you are living in this moment. Always allow your heart to guide you, and make choices based on joy and love for yourSelf—selfLove. And know that the result will be a greater experience of joy in all the glorious moments of your life.

What two behaviors or choices do you most want to change in your life?

What choices do you need to make to change these behaviors?

Choose a friend to share this with and ask them to help you live up to your commitment to change your behavior.

CHAPTER THREE

The Challenge—Healing Through Love

You are what you believe. You live your choices.
And you are responsible for everything that is of your life!

All healing occurs through love...and the most powerful love we can experience is selfLove. By acknowledging and embracing this truth in our hearts, we can experience our lives in greater peace and joy than we could imagine.

We are powerful Beings, yet we feel helpless in the face of adversity. We often believe that things happen *to* us, rather than recognizing that we bring forth our experiences in all moments—moments of joy as well as moments of pain.

Prior to my experience with cancer, I thought I was living a joyful life. The adversities that had presented themselves to me over the years were always overcome, and life was peaceful. I was eating healthfully and working in a new realm, as a medical intuitive, with great joy. I had moved to Colorado, which had been a dream my husband and I shared for many years. My daughters had been easy children to raise and were wonderful young women. I had many loving friends and felt blessed.

But still, I created powerful illness in my body. Why?

It took a long time for me to face my truth—that I did not love mySelf. I easily became frustrated when things didn't go "just right." I judged mySelf harshly, criticizing my hair, my body, the cleanliness of my home, and even my work (was I good enough?). I sought the approval of others and felt betrayed if I was criticized or challenged for my choices. I nagged my husband and my children, expecting perfect behavior from them as well as from mySelf. And I kept mySelf private—and separate from others—deep in my heart.

This is not the behavior of a person experiencing selfLove.

Once I discovered that I could "choose" to love and celebrate mySelf, my personal world changed...and it has affected the lives of those closest to me. My body let go of the energies of pain it had been holding onto for so long, allowing powerful healing to take place. I found peace for mySelf and have learned to allow all others their choices in their own hearts and lives. I have let go of my personal requirements for perfection, recognizing that everything that exists is perfect as it is. I see mySelf with acceptance for all that I am, and I now share love with others with a depth I never before experienced.

I experienced more than the healing of my cancer; I experienced the healing of my heart and life.

This book is a journey into the discovery of total healing. There is no Being upon this planet who is unable to create the experience of total well-being for himSelf or herSelf. We are all alike as humans, and yet we each make choices of separation from one another...and often from ourSelves. As we learn to accept and embrace ourSelves in total selfLove, we recognize our perfection and create harmony in all states of our Being, physical, emotional and spiritual.

There is a powerful basic truth that I put forth with these words: all healing occurs through love of Self. We have been taught that selfLove is selfish, but this is not the case. By loving oneSelf, a person is capable of sharing even greater love with all others. We cannot love another unconditionally unless we love ourSelves in that manner. For example, as much as a parent may love a child, that love is limited if the parent does not love and honor him or herSelf powerfully and profoundly.

So, how do we choose selfLove?

By choosing to celebrate with love and joy who we are! By recognizing that we are wonderful and magnificent in all moments of our lives. By learning through acknowledgment that sometimes our actions bring forth pain and by releasing self-judgment for these actions. By seeing our beauty in all moments and reflecting this beauty to the world. By taking responsibility for each thought and each action and by moving from each moment of choice into the next one, recognizing that we create change simply by choosing to.

We are each all-powerful! Each thought we have creates our experience. We are *responsible* for every aspect of our lives, including our relationships, our state of abundance, our emotional reactions to others and our physical health. We are always making choices, even when we believe we are not. Making *no* choice is a choice, and ultimately creates an experience for which we are responsible.

We should not spend our lives blaming others for the circumstances of our personal experiences. We can choose to take action...or not. We can choose to make changes...or not. We are never helpless, although, in many instances, we believe that we are, and therefore, our choices lead us to behaviors of powerlessness. Our lives are filled with as much abundance or as much lack as we believe, and the manifestation of our beliefs lead us into that experience of truth. You are what you believe. You live your choices. And you are responsible for everything that is of your life!

Once responsibility is acknowledged, profound changes occur within an individual. Those with emotional issues involving another person can choose to recognize that they are playing the victim role in the given relationship, joining in a dance of pain. By accepting the perfection of all, they can then look at the issues that paralyzed them with a new perspective, knowing that even though the antagonist may not change, they themSelves have the freedom to refuse to continue to dance. And who wants to dance alone? Conflicts can easily come to an end whenever one partner refuses to dance the dance that creates the experience of powerlessness.

In all moments, as we make new choices, things change. With physical issues, when people accept and acknowledge their perfection, they choose to assist and partner with the doctor, because they acknowledge their own responsibility in all moments and thereby create the perfect path for themSelves. Additionally, the healing is usually achieved more quickly and easily when one's perfection is acknowledged because there are no longer thoughts or words of self-diminishment.

A side effect of the experience of selfLove is freedom. Freedom to Be. Freedom to live without fear, guilt, rules or pain. Freedom from the limitation created through the belief that we are weak and powerless. Freedom to recognize and know our own magnificence. Freedom to love all others without needing to hold them tightly, for in freedom there is no fear of aloneness and no fear of danger. There is the recognition that all experience is created by ourSelves, in order to grow into even greater freedom...and greater love.

Those who choose selfLove and freedom rarely create illness within their bodies, because they allow themSelves the experience to freely flow as all that they are. But that is not to say that a person without illness is one who is free! Illness is not always that which is apparent in the physical body. Dis-ease can be emotional, preventing the free, joyous flow of life. You may know someone who is "healthy as a horse," but who is mean-spirited or just plain unhappy. The blocks are there, but the manifestation of pain is not in the physical body. The healing is as important here as it is in one who has created a physical manifestation of illness, for the heart is experiencing lack of selfLove and powerful limitation. Without selfLove, you do not experience freedom—or joy—as fully. When you live in selfLove, you experience the fullness of your life.

We can choose to recognize who we are in *all* moments. We are perfect. We are powerful. We are love. When we accept this Truth, we then begin to fully live. Otherwise, as time progresses, the limitations we perceive in our environment—family, school, religion, government, jobs—become a wall separating us from experiencing ourSelves. The perfection is always there. As is the love. But we are separated from this experience. How many of us teach our children to be afraid? How many of us judge others because of our own fears? How many of us feel unworthy to be the wonderful Beings that we are? And how can we, as humans, overcome everything that has been taught to us time and again, leaving us powerless to gain control of the reins of our Truth? *Our very lives are at stake!*

We can choose to release the limitations that we have chosen to embrace by first recognizing that we have the freedom to do so! We can choose to acknowledge our own responsibility for our lives and understand that each person in our lives—our parents, our children, our employers, our friends—are the teachers whom we have called forth to allow us to come to the knowing that we are magnificent! That we are free! That we are love! That we are powerful!

⋰⋰⋱⋱

We live in the simplest of all times, yet we create complications concerning all things. We live in extraordinary times, yet we create the most ordinary in our routines. And we live in a time of great understanding, although most remain blind to all that they know. This is a story about my journey in this lifetime, a journey which has led me to the simple, yet extraordinary understanding of the power of Self, the power of love, the power of healing.

This is my story. It is a story not unlike most, for it is simply a path I chose in order to manifest into what I am now. It is a story of family dysfunction and pain, and a story of reward and joy. It is an ordinary path, and a perfect path, for it has led me to the discovery of selfLove and personal magnificence. It is similar to the path of many, but through choice and work and desire, this path—*my* path—has brought me to total self-healing.

While sharing my story, I clearly indicate where the emotional reactions to my early life created energy blocks and how these energies impacted my life. I also guide you to understand how I chose to release these same energies, to bring me to the joyful life I am now experiencing. And it is my desire that these words will awaken within you the same desire to make choices which will bring you to the recognition of your perfection and the experience of your own healing.

Allow these pages to awaken within you the truth of the magnificence of your Self. Choose to be empowered, so that you can then acknowledge and honor the energies that offer you the wondrous experience of discovering who you are, ultimately guiding you to experience peace, joy and great health. Read these words and let them curl up within your heart, for the memory of who you are lies dormant within your Being. Awaken and open your heart and, from this moment forth, free yourSelf of the beliefs which manifest the limitations and pain you experience. Heal yourSelf with love.

If you now choose, from here your healing begins.

CHAPTER FOUR

My Story

We each have a story to share as we journey through this lifetime, and yet most of us are reluctant to speak.

As adults, we sense that there is little value in discussing the things that happened long ago, and yet we hold on to those very experiences which we do not wish to honor by giving them our voice. And so, whenever I do my work, I always begin by asking each person to share their story...and I honor the story, for it leads to the discovery of how the person created their experiences and led them to this moment in their lives.

Through free will and choice, all personal experiences create a package that we call *personality*, and we can recognize that, as we free ourSelves by simply speaking of our personal history, we change aspects of Self which directly affect our personality—how we react, what we feel, choices we make. It is important to begin by knowing that, once the story has been told and these old energies are released, it becomes a closed chapter. There is no reason to rehash memories time and again, for holding on to the pain of long ago simply locks us in that moment of experience, rather than enabling us to experience the present moment. We can choose to honor who we were in childhood and young adulthood, release the limitations which were created there, and then continue the creation of a new story of our lives!

In sharing my story, not only do I have a forum to free myself of that which is no longer, but I can also show you how I manifested pain in my body, which ultimately led to my experience of cancer. By sharing my personal history, I also offer all others the opportunity to recognize that, just as I have told my story, the stories of all can be shared in trust and love, enabling a great many the freedom to finally Be who they truly are, in this moment and always.

⋇⋇⋇⋇

Through much of my life, my mother shared with me the horrendous story of my birth—how I refused to be born, while she was tied up on a birthing table and left alone for hours, screaming in pain. This was her truth and it became mine, allowing energies of guilt to permeate me at a young age.

When I finally passed through the birthing canal, I came upon the scene feet first, further complicating the process. I know now, through my inner sense, that my soul was quite reluctant to come into physical existence upon the Earth, but for reasons unknown to me for most of my life, I had a mission which I was to carry out.

I was not an easy child to begin family life with. My parents, both Holocaust survivors, were new to the United States, having emigrated from France shortly after the war. I was born with two clubbed feet and a topsy-turvy intestinal tract, which prevented food from being digested properly. My parents were very poor, and had little means to support a sickly baby.

However, in total perfection, my parents were led to wonderful doctors, who were able to restructure the bones of my feet and clear up my intestinal tract. My mother reports that I was able to walk normally before the age of one, and that, by age three, I was physically healthy on all counts, my digestive tract finally permitting me to gain weight and reach a normal size.

I was not born of love; I was created in fear. The Korean War had broken out, and my father, a newly-sworn American citizen, was afraid of being drafted. My parents believed that men were exempt if they had children, and so I joined my family simply in an effort for my father to avoid the draft.

My parents were truly unprepared in all ways to have a child, for they were still learning the language and ways of America. I was raised in a multilingual household, intermingling French, Yiddish and English in my speech. My father was a tailor working in a Manhattan sweatshop, paid by the piece; my mother's job as a seamstress ended at my birth. We lived in a small apartment in the Bronx, New York City, in what I call a ghetto, for it was a neighborhood of mostly Jewish immigrants with some Italians and Irish thrown in, creating ethnic diversity.

My parents were an interesting couple. My father and his entire family had come to the United States, and although they were close, there was severe dysfunction. My grandmother was a widow who demanded that her children take care of her, and my father, aunt and uncle felt burdened but obligated to do so. They had all survived the war and had come to the United States penniless. My mother, on the other hand, came from a wealthy family and survived the war through the wealth of her father, who "bought" the family's freedom from the Nazis time and time again.

My mother met my father as a young teenager during the war, and their paths remained intertwined throughout those years. She was a beautiful girl, full of fire, which attracted my shy, quiet father. She was not really interested in him and broke his heart more than once. My mother had been severely physically abused

Go back in time and remember a joyous childhood memory.

What made it joyful? Bring to mind a painful or fearful memory as well.

Look at these experiences and examine how they have impacted you, affecting your present beliefs and life choices.

by her father, a large hulking man who was once a boxer. When my father left France for the United States, my mother saw the possibility of great freedom and followed him here. Once married, she was abandoned by her family, who looked scornfully upon her choice, and she was left isolated and without the wealth to which she had become accustomed.

And so I was born into this unhappiness. I have memories of childhood that date back to the age of three. In this European family, there was a rule that children were to be seen and not heard, and so I was silenced as a child.

My mother's abusive history was brought forth into her parenting, and both my sister, born four years after me, and I endured severe physical as well as emotional abuse. Looking back at photos taken when I was a child, I see that I was always perfectly clean and coifed, never allowed to play in the mud, let alone get rumpled and dirtied. My father, who was already emotionally beaten down by his own mother, usually quietly retreated during my mother's outbursts, allowing his children to suffer the brunt of her rage.

As in all situations, there were also moments of happiness in my young life. My immigrant parents enjoyed exploring the museums and sights of New York City, and we all enjoyed these special occasions. My favorite pastime, however, was to immerse myself in books, for, through reading, I could escape into the adventures of the characters. I always imagined myself to be the heroine of each story and truly loved fairy tales or biographies in which the woman was the focus. Bible stories were a special favorite and, as I grew older, I loved the myths and legends of all cultures.

Deep within my core, I believed that all the magic depicted in these stories had to be real in some way and felt that, once I knew the secrets, I could create this same magic! In fact, ever since I was very young, I remember wishing that, when I grew up, I would have the perfect family—a husband who loved me just as I was and two beautiful and perfect children who would adore me forever! Little did I know the power and magic of that creation!

When we were very young, my sister and I were sent off to bed at an unusually early hour, so my parents could have the evening alone. I was never tired, and I was not allowed to read in bed but rather was told to sleep. I learned to create a fantasy in my mind which enabled the time to pass until slumber took over. I imagined that God was my "daddy" and that I could simply run into his arms and be with him for as long as I liked, watching angels come and go and universal decisions unfold. As I got older, this fantasy enabled me to be granted "powers" (after all, when God is your daddy, you can do everything!) and for years, I continued to be the heroine of my own imagination.

I look back at these fantasies with great fondness. I felt protected...and perfect! God never judged me, never reprimanded me or punished me. I was beautiful, intelligent and powerful, and I used my power for the good of mankind.

My adventures became more and more involved and, as I grew up, so did my fantasy life. Never for a moment did I imagine that this fantasy was real. Never would I dare to think that I was all those things that I created for myself—beautiful, intelligent or powerful! It was as though I were living two lives, and my fantasy life was a joyful one!

In my everyday life, however, I was always reminded that I was far from perfect. I powerfully remember hearing time and again that my sister was the "pretty one" and I was the "smart one." How homely I felt! And how driven I was to succeed in school, in order to uphold this image my parents had of me! My driving fear was that, if I did poorly in school, they would stop loving me, for then I would have no positive attributes at all. And so, my school experience, albeit an academically successful one, was unhappy, as well, for I did not allow mySelf the freedom to explore *me*! I never rebelled or experimented with clothing or makeup or hair colors. I only wore the clothing my mother purchased and never went shopping alone or with girlfriends. I was the classic nerd, with a total focus on grades and competition.

I have now come to my teen years, offering you insight into my life. One can surmise from the experiences shared that I became quiet and reserved, desperately trying to avoid attracting attention to myself. I was self-conscious and placed great pressure upon myself to be perfect, for that was what was expected of me.

I was afraid of my mother and, although I had idolized my quiet father in my childhood, I had come to realize that his meekness and silence were choices to not protect me, and so I learned to trust no one in my life. My "spirit" was essentially beaten out of me, and I buried myself in the world of books and the adventures of characters both real and fictional, wishing for their lives, rather than my own. I did not know how to "live" and became like my father.

Would we call this a genetically created personality? I think not, for I could have lived so much more than he, had I made different choices. My mother simply followed the path of her own upbringing by raising her children in an environment similar to the one she was raised in; my father, who felt powerless because of his childhood, remained in that state.

Now the challenge: my parents *chose* to be the kind of parents they were. My mother could have changed her methods of parenting, had she loved *herSelf* enough to do so, and because she did not, she could give us no more love than she had for herSelf!

Also, my father could have protected my sister and me, had he had the self-empowerment to do so, but his lack of selfLove created the paralysis of his life. Although my sister and I were the victims of this abuse, I also know that, at a soul level, we chose this family in order to learn, and teach, great lessons.

And what of the extended family—the grandparents, aunts, uncles and cousins, who were witness to the abuse we children endured? Why was there silence? Why was the fear of confronting the abuser greater than the love for the abused? How could I see myself with any importance in the eyes of anyone, if everyone chose to look upon me with eyes that refused to see my truth? It amazes me how many people have influence over the health and well-being of a child. We must never limit the responsibility to the parents;

we should each examine our roles as human beings and choose to protect *all* children from abuse or neglect!

In my adult years, I separately confronted my grandmother, an aunt and an uncle and asked them why they had done nothing to protect my sister and myself. The answers were the same: they didn't want to rock the boat; they didn't want to appear disrespectful to my parents; they didn't think it was their business; it didn't seem so bad.

How bad is bad? What does it take for us, as a society, to honor our children? When will we understand the importance of raising our families with unconditional love and respect for each as individuals?

And so, I present to you the personality I had through a great part of my life. I was distrustful, which prevented me from easily making or holding on to friendships; I was limited in my ability to share love, since I hardly loved mySelf at all; I was unable to form personal opinions about anything, since I was always told what and how to think; and I was terribly shy, creating the aura of invisibility I needed in order to avoid my mother's wrath.

By contrast, my sister reacted quite differently to a parallel childhood. She left home at age seventeen, dabbled with alcohol and drugs and used sex as a means of getting attention, love and confirmation that she existed. She was the opposite of shy, always speaking her mind and challenging the world around her. It took her many years to create her present, more peaceful life, but her years of self-created turmoil were the reflection and backlash of her feelings of frustration and powerlessness.

To make matters worse, I had spent much time allowing my sister to receive further abuse because of my internal rage. For many years, I tormented her physically and emotionally, needing an outlet and never recognizing that, rather than finding strength in our unity, I expressed my power through her helplessness. How sad for us both, since it has taken many years for a relationship to form as the result of the poison of our young lives.

My high school years were very challenging, in that it was the '60s, and for a shy, frightened young girl, the freedom of the hippie culture was quite a shock. As I was unused to formulating my own opinions, I carried forth my parents' disdain and made it my own. I was fortunate in being able to attend New York City's prestigious High School of Music and Art, the only reward for the terrible hours of piano study I had endured for the previous eight years.

In order to attend this school, I needed to travel over an hour each way, by bus and subway, into a world quite unlike the one I had grown up in. In this environment, I came face to face with a subculture of talent, experimentation and freedom, with young artists and musicians from all over the city coming together with the desire to grow and expand in realms beyond my limited imagination. And it is here where I began to grow up and change, bringing challenges home because I wanted to fit in with those whom I admired from afar. Arguments in my home escalated, and my mother's outbursts had less and less of an effect upon me, since I was finally able to physically look her in the eyes, limiting her desire to reach out and strike.

It was during this time that I suddenly noticed the opposite sex and, although I was forbidden to date, I had my share of flirtations. My dreams changed from the adventures of others within the books of my youth into the creation of my own happiness.

Still tethered to the apron strings of home, I attended the City College of New York, receiving a college education without the independence of dormitory life. I was a good student and, during these years, I mastered the ability to regurgitate the information sought by professors and teachers, rather than expressing my rather different ways of analyzing the myriad of literary works I was drawn to read through my class choices. Even here, I quickly learned to withhold my truth and simply agree with those who were in charge of that moment of my life. I felt powerless in my childhood and never learned that I could take it back in a moment.

In the latter part of my freshman year, I met Hank. He was an unusual young man, different from all the others I had been dating. He had an uncontrolled smile, the reflection of an inner joy I could not understand. He exuded a confidence which masked issues of unworthiness, but to my naive and untrained, youthful eyes, I simply saw the presentation he offered to the outside world.

And I was smitten.

Following a volatile and emotional courtship, we married while I was still attending college. Looking back, I can see that we both were quite young and inexperienced, but chose this path as a means of escaping our difficult home lives.

If you ask me about my wedding, I can share with you the memory of the day itself, which was glorious, but nothing about the plans and preparations. My parents took complete charge, without any input from the bride or groom.

I accepted this situation, for this was simply the continuation of the way my life had been controlled. I never enjoyed the experience of choosing my wedding dress, or even of trying on more than the one I ultimately wore. My parents walked in one day with a dress that had been worn by a neighbor's daughter, and I simply tried it on. Since it fit me perfectly, it was purchased, and that was all there was to it.

I was easy-going and anxious to please, but I was also accustomed to accepting all things that were presented to me, never for a moment even knowing that perhaps I wanted a different experience.

Needless to say, this created conflict when Hank and I went out to purchase our first pieces of furniture. When we excitedly shared our joy at finding a bedroom set we loved or our first dinette table, my parents were outraged! How could we make such major choices without their input? They would know best what we liked, of course, plus they could get us better prices, because they knew how to shop around, etc.

Fortunately for me, Hank quite firmly claimed *our* independence and freedom, over and over again, until they began to back off on issues involving him. Naturally, they still worked on me whenever possible, and in situations which did not include Hank. And I allowed it to be.

The years that followed were filled with experiences which brought me into opportunities for great learning. During these years, we bore two magnificent daughters, each having chosen us to guide them along their glorious pathways of perfection. These angels were, and still are, among our greatest teachers of this lifetime.

As a new mother, I was truly in my glory! I could never have imagined such profound love for another Being! The birth of our first-born, Jodi, was a joy, so much so that the obstetrician, a young doctor, asked permission to include his wife in the delivery room, so that she could watch her husband at work. There was much celebration as this cherub came forth, never crying and with wide open, knowing eyes.

Funny thing—the fact that Jodi never cried became a source of concern for me in those early days. Whoever heard of such a non-fussy baby? A week after her birth, in my concern that something was amiss, I scratched the bottoms of her feet in order to hear her wail. Why did I not simply accept the perfection of Jodi as she was? Why was I looking for something "wrong?" Why did I choose to create pain upon the body of this angel in order to assuage my own fears?

Of course, Jodi had nothing wrong with her, but for years I was the same as most, always looking at my child with an inner fear that something could be wrong or go wrong. What fears are we, as parents, creating in the hearts of our children...and in our *own* hearts?

There is a moment in my parenting that I always remember with deep regret; yet it is a life-changing moment, granting me an opportunity to make a choice which would affect the rest of my life.

I was a very strict and rigid parent; although loving my child fully, I demanded perfection from her with an adult's mind and heart. What we can learn to do as parents is simply become the child, and then choose to allow the child the freedom of Being, of exploration, of dirt and toys and questions and total experience. As adults, we create horrendous limitations upon our children, stripping them of the wings they were born with to fly in total joy.

In those early years, I was a mother not much different from my own. My demands upon my daughter were no different from my mother's demands on me. One day, for reasons long forgotten, I found myself straddling a fallen two-year old who was crying in fear of my upswung hand, which was about to come down to hit her. In that instant, I saw mySelf from outside of mySelf, almost as though I were looking at a still-life photo. I froze in horror. It was one of the longest moments of my life, and I suddenly knew that I wanted to break the behavior pattern I was creating between mySelf and my child.

I wrapped Jodi in my arms and rocked her for a long time, crying my requests for her forgiveness and accepting her little hand's rubbing my cheek in total love. There was a long road of healing yet before me, and I made many choices which placed limitations upon my children, but never again in my life did I lose control at the risk of creating harm to anyone, including mySelf. I recognized the power I had as a mother, and I chose never again to abuse it in rage.

⊰⊱⊰⊱

It is of great importance to pause at this moment of my story to point out that all of these actions and energies are of long ago. We can look back upon our childhood and, in many cases, find cause for pain, for rage, for present-life dysfunction. It is powerfully important to understand that the circumstances of our lives follow pathways that allow us to be who we are *in this moment*, and the perfection of our personal history leads us to the perfection of this moment of our lives, such as it is.

Many people grow up in dysfunctional families but still continue to function well in society. Continuing the dysfunction is easy, for we *allow* what has been in our lives to stay with us, unless we choose to let go of our pain and judgment of Self and others. In my case, I have learned that who

I am in this moment would be different, if not for the experiences of my childhood. And since I love who I am, was my childhood not perfect?

In any moment that we experience lack of selfLove, is it because of a childhood trauma or is it because of a present-moment circumstance? How long do we choose to hold on to pain, if pain does not honor us? How long do we choose to punish our parents, our spouses, ourSelves, for a moment in time that is no longer *this* moment? Rather, why not simply ride the waves of Being and allow the Self to take hold of the responsibility of who we are *now*, not worrying about the pathways of how we have arrived? It is time to accept that we are living *this* moment...and that no other moment exists, once we let go and allow life to flow.

In my own personal healing process, I struggled with letting go—letting go of painful memories, letting go of feelings of betrayal, distrust and lack of unconditional love. I can, if I choose, continue to hold on to the issues of my youth. I can choose to continue to blame my insecurities and imperfections on my past. I can choose to look backwards as I experience this moment in my life. But what would this bring me, other than energies focused on less than the perfection of who I am? Wouldn't these choices limit my experience of being all that I am?

Change is constant. As I have changed, so have the people of my youth. My mother, now a widow, has created a life for herSelf which is joy-filled and honorable. She is loved by her peers and is giving and generous in countless ways. She loves her children and her grandchildren as well and as powerfully as she is able, within the confines of her self-created limitations and lack of selfLove. She still struggles with insecurity and fear, and is slowly recognizing that letting go is challenging...while I remind her that, when she chooses to do so, the rewards will be great.

And as she changes, will *I* not change? Why hold on to the memory of who she was, rather than embrace who she *is*? If I ask others to accept me as I am in *this* moment, should I not accept them for who they are in this moment, as well? It is honoring not to hold on to who we think someone is, simply because that is who they once were. Rather, we can gift each other, and ourSelves, with the freedom to be different...and with this freedom, all change becomes possible.

⫷⫸

The early years of our marriage were quite challenging for our small family. We had made the choice to move from New York City to a suburb of New Jersey, creating for Hank a tedious daily commute back and forth to Manhattan for a few years. I was surrounded by other newly-implanted New Yorkers whose financial situations were stronger than our own, and became caught up in the games of who has more than whom, how much things cost, what kind of car you drive, what designer labels the kids wear, expensive weekend activities and the like.

During this time in my life, I was miserable...and was making home life miserable for everyone. I wanted to have all those things everyone else had! My parents had always been keen on current styles and what the neighbors thought, so I simply fell into this same way of living. Although surrounded all day long by people with young children, I did not recognize my loneliness. I was lonely because I did not fit in. I was lonely because I had little in common with these "friends." I was lonely mostly because I did not know who I was...and if I had, I would have chosen to be alone and I would never have been lonely!

I have learned that being alone and being lonely are not the same thing. In fact, the truth is that we are *never* alone! We are always connected to *all that is!* What we can do as humans is to allow this truth to filter through our minds and past the choice to see ourselves as separate. We are *all people!* We are *all things!* We are magnificent Beings, grander than we can even fathom! And with this acceptance, we find that we are never alone!

Loneliness, on the other hand, can occur even when in a crowd. Have you ever gone to a gathering of family, or co-workers, or even friends, and spent hours on small-talk, all the while feeling isolated within yourSelf, wishing you were someplace else? You were certainly not alone, but the loneliness was the result of your choice to feel separate, and as though you were simply wasting your time. And in a sense, you were, because you allowed yourSelf the choice of joining a group that did not bring you joy. We all have freedom of choice, and we all can learn how to make choices which honor us.

Back then, I did not recognize that I had the choice to be myself, just as I was. I wanted to fit in. I wanted to be like everyone else. I did not know who I was, so I had no self-image of worth or value. I mimicked those around me, and I diminished myself as compared to those people who occupied my environment. Whose fault was this? No one's. It was simply my *choice*. And, as a result, I experienced loneliness and unhappiness.

Jodi was two-and-a-half years old when our lives were suddenly thrown into chaos by my father's unexpected diagnosis of colon cancer. There was hysteria all around, since he was the center of the extended family, a man quite beloved by his siblings, his nieces and nephews, as well as by all of us. He underwent surgery, and the doctor assured us that the cancer had been removed. We never questioned the fact that he was not offered the option of chemotherapy, and we were all happy to move past this difficult time.

Soon after my father's challenging experience, I felt the desire to have our second child. Almost immediately after discovering I was pregnant, I miscarried and was devastated. We were told to wait three months before trying again and, once again, I conceived easily and was elated. One day, during my first trimester, I was with some friends and was playing with a child who had been inoculated with the Rubella vaccine earlier that day. Within two days, I was covered with a rash from head to toe. Alarmed, I made an emergency appointment with my obstetrician, who sent me immediately to an allergist. The prognosis was serious: I had the German measles!

I returned to the obstetrician's office in tears, and was given the statistics regarding the risks to having a healthy birth. Paralyzed with fear, I simply looked into the doctor's eyes and asked him what I should do. It was illegal for him to tell me, so I asked him what advice he would give me if I were carrying his grandchild. His answer was sincere and direct. He would tell his daughter that she was healthy and would have many more children. We scheduled the abortion for later that week.

The reactions of people to this choice were amazing. Every person had an opinion, even though I asked for none. I was in mourning, having desperately wanted another child. This was not a decision made on a whim! Oddly enough, my greatest critic was the mother of the child with whom I had played on that fateful day of her inoculation. For once, I acknowledged my power and chose to end our friendship, as the result of her judgment of me and my private actions.

I easily conceived again three months later. Dara's birth was one of great joy. She came into this world wailing lustily and was an inquisitive child who never stopped talking. She adored her older sister, and I made every effort to allow them to establish the friendship they enjoy to this day. Jodi was the perfect older sibling, caring for her baby sister with great joy. Their healthy arguments have always been few and far between, and they honor each other fully. They created a bond in unity, and when I was angry with either one, they both stood together before me, their brave little faces defending each other with a fierce protectiveness I never experienced in my own childhood. This brought me great joy, and although I lost my temper on many occasions, the choices I made in parenting these girls are long past, and I totally accept and honor them all. Children are resilient, flourishing in all moments when they are raised with unconditional love and the respect they deserve.

The years went by comfortably, until my father had a relapse of the colon cancer. It had metastasized into his liver, which was at that time a death knell. Chemotherapy was his chosen means of cure, and he also changed his diet to aid his recovery. During this time, Hank was fiercely exploring alternative therapies, but my father stubbornly stayed with the medical pathways, unwilling to try methods he did not intellectually accept.

His passing came quickly, which was a blessing. However, as his disease grew and his strength weakened, he experienced such anger that his entire personality was changed during his last weeks. My father never believed in God, and he found no peace within himSelf, nor through prayer. In fact, while in the hospice a few days before he died, he literally threw out a rabbi who came to speak with him. My father died a very angry man.

⊰⊱⊱⊰

The years following my father's death were years of great change for all members of my family. The years were uneventful and life continued, although Hank made choices which affected us all quite profoundly.

Through most of the years of our marriage, Hank was always voraciously reading any and all books he could find on many aspects of spirituality. He tried to share his expanded beliefs with me, but I was afraid of much of what he believed. He had lost interest in those things most people discuss— politics, sports and the like. He was finding people who were also following this path, and our circle of friends began to fall apart.

We were traveling in different spaces and, for quite some time, I was afraid that our marriage would not survive his personal quest. I refused to allow him to have his strange conversations with family or friends; on the way to gatherings with others, I would list subjects he would not be allowed to discuss during that evening. I was controlling him, not allowing him the freedom he yearned to experience. I am eternally grateful that he loved me so dearly, for surely, had this not been the case, we would have separated long ago.

Years passed before I began to read the books Hank had been leaving out as enticement. I became mesmerized, reading all of Ruth Montgomery's books, followed by the Seth series. I was taken by Barbara Marciniak's writings and suddenly realized that I was hooked! I was resonating with the messages these books presented to me. To Hank's great joy, I came home excited and filled with questions. Dinner table conversations were lively, and soon our girls were caught up in the possibilities of life beyond the physical experience. Yes, they thought it was "weird," but they, too, began to ask questions and were always ready and willing to accept truths that went beyond the norm.

As time moved forward, Hank became interested in a form of healing called Spiritual Response Therapy (SRT). Spiritual Response Therapy is a healing modality which researches the Akashic Record (the history of each person's soul) to uncover lifetimes of energies which have not been fully released. By releasing them through this process, the person is able more fully to embrace this lifetime with joy and peace, as well as to release energies creating unnecessary discord and illness.

In fact, Hank's SRT practice was becoming so successful that, as soon as he worked with one person, he would get requests from family members and friends of that person, creating a backlog of healing work which forced people to wait three to four weeks for his time. As a result, Hank was spending more and more time performing this healing work and gradually chose to do this full-time.

The backlog became so great that, in order to manage the work, the time came for me to assist Hank in this endeavor. We would sit for three or four hours each day, doing the SRT together, even though I was never formally trained in the process. As time progressed, we discovered that I had the ability to "read" the records intuitively, rather than needing to explore the details through the more mechanical methods taught through the SRT process.

In fact, while working on one client, we came across a lifetime in which I suddenly "saw" a throng of angry people carrying torches and marching towards a small cottage. They were after a woman whom they claimed was practicing witchcraft. I "saw" her being dragged from her home, while her children were screaming, and she was burned to death. It was frightening for me to "relive" this experience, even as an observer, and I soon learned to filter the images, so that there was no sound and so that I would have no emotional reaction to the experience. This was the beginning of my spiritual expansion, and it was joyous!

Hank was in the habit of meditating twice each day, choosing to do so in order to increase his healing abilities. Most times, I would join him in this silence, not knowing what I was doing but simply allowing mySelf to "be." After many weeks, I was suddenly aware of images before me, as though a television were turned on inside my head. I felt a strange sensation in my body, rather tingly and expansive. I did not know what this was, but it was a comfortable feeling, and so I stayed silent. Suddenly the top of my head felt as if it was opening up, and a part of me was growing larger from my inside! As I grew in height and width, I felt the sensation of angel wings touching me all over. Although I did not quite understand the significance of that moment, I was in a state of supreme awe at the experience, my heart bursting wide open in great joy. It was the birthing of the new me.

Needless to say, I looked forward to our meditations. Through the images that were presented to me, I was shown my truth on many levels. I was shown my path and the paths of the people closest to my heart. I would share with Hank and the girls images about them, and they were always fascinated and excited. I soon learned that, if I asked questions, I would receive answers, and it was fun to receive information about things both mundane and esoteric.

One day, Jodi was sitting and meditating beside me when she quietly asked if I could get answers to *her* questions. I had no idea whether that was possible, but I decided to try. She began asking questions regarding choices which were before her, and suddenly I heard mySelf "flowing" the information she needed! What was interesting about all of this is that I had absolutely no memory of anything I said, but when I was finished and I opened my eyes, she was glowing, her eyes bright with an inner acceptance of the information.

It was then that I was able to "see" that the path of my life was about to change. It was also then when I realized that my words would create great impact in the hearts and minds of people who would come to me for such readings. I felt compelled to take a "Vow of Truth," that is, that any word I spoke would only be of total and absolute truth, regardless of the circumstances.

This was not an easy vow to make, for it involved conscious participation. I would not only speak truth when doing a "reading" for a client, but when involved with any person at any time, including mySelf. I recognized that people have a tendency to hide from themSelves, as I had been doing in my *own* life. It is not always easy to be honest with your*Self*, let alone others! It is hard to admit that perhaps in self-judgment, we see ourSelves as a bit greedy, or selfish or even unhappy. We hide this from Self and others, but by doing so, we are simply building walls around our hearts. It was important to me to have an open heart, and I did all that I could to live my life in truth and honesty.

And so I began to do spiritual readings. I practiced for quite some time on my immediate family and my closest friends. I was not yet comfortable coming out of the closet, so to speak. This was truly not a path I had ever dreamt for mySelf, nor one that many people would accept seriously.

To "legitimize" mySelf, I became accredited as a hypnotherapist, allowing for greater expansion of my work in the healing venue. I began to specialize in past-life regression, which I discovered was a fun and powerful healing tool. So, like Hank, my work began to build via word of mouth, and soon I, too, became quite busy.

Throughout this transition within my life, I was always wanting to learn more, grow more, experience more. I was curious regarding my future pathway and my life purpose here on Earth, having learned through sessions with clients and guided by their questions that there is more here than meets the eye. I began my own personal "conversation with God," if you will. Quite often, I would close mySelf in my room and powerfully speak aloud my desire to gain more knowing, more insight...even more power! I did not really understand what I was doing, but I did recognize that shortly after these private "conversations," something within me would change. The depth of my inner vision increased, my personal peace expanded and I experienced great joy.

Personal meditations became more powerful, and I gradually made dietary changes which, in turn, allowed my physical vibrations to accept more easily the energies which were flowing through me. Initially, I was struggling with headaches, dizziness and other mild symptoms created by the energetic shifts I was allowing to happen; as I chose to eliminate caffeine, sugar and red meat, these symptoms passed and I was stronger. To this day, I still make further changes to my lifestyle. As I honor my own inner "knowing," the joy and ease of my work increases multi-fold!

As time progressed, I discovered that, as I gave guidance through psychic readings, I would also be guided to identify blocks within the person for whom I was doing the reading. I was then guided to offer suggestions regarding physical weaknesses, or nutritional imbalances, or other challenges. This process came slowly, and I had to totally trust the information as well as mySelf, for this could powerfully impact the person hearing these truths. I never offered the information if it was not requested, and if I felt compelled to speak without the person's permission, I was always stopped either by a sudden cough, a sneeze or an interruption. I quickly learned the importance of honoring an individual's readiness to hear the truth. If they were ready, they sought greater information. If they were not ready, I honored their choice.

There was great joy in doing this work, but I still had disharmony in my life. I had difficulty with my extended family and over the years continued to be either ignored or ridiculed for the choices made by both Hank and mySelf. Our daughters were embarrassed by the work we did, and when asked about their parents' vocations, continued to speak about Hank's engineering in water technology and my marketing and advertising jobs. It took them quite some time to come to the full acceptance of our chosen field. In their late teens, as they grew to understand our choices, they were able to freely share the truth of our work.

And so, as my work continued, I found mySelf able to teach people, one at a time, their ability to receive their own information through meditative flow. This was the most joyous time for me, for I was now able to share the energies of connection, thereby spreading peace and harmony for each of them to maintain on their own, by their own choosing. As I brought individuals into connection, I began to realize that this was beginning to change the energies of the Earth—perhaps only a trickle at a time, but nonetheless with a heart filled with expectation that change was upon us all!

Time flew by quickly, with my work and gifts expanding simultaneously. I was beginning to recognize the power of my ability to "see." One of our clients was a young man who had suffered from severe, chronic headaches since his college days. Hank spent much time working with this client, and although the headaches eased, they were not totally gone. I worked with him as well, and was surprised to find that he drank lots of water and maintained a healthy diet. However, once merged with his energy, I was suddenly faced with a personal truth: that at some point in college he had "date-raped" a young woman, and had been suffering from guilt ever since. Hence, the headaches.

This was quite an interesting realization for me. How to approach this without evoking rage...and how could I possibly know that I was right? I spoke with him carefully about this and, sad to say, we never heard from him again. I would never know for sure if I was right, but I *do* know that I pushed a button in his heart which held some level of truth, for he never denied what I saw.

Working with people in this way is quite challenging at times. Many people only want to hear information which confirms that they are "right" in their way of viewing the world. One of my clients was a woman who was very unhappy in her life. Carol,* recently divorced, had custody of her abusive teenagers, who blamed her for their unhappiness. She also had financial difficulties resulting from a poor divorce settlement. Although Carol got to keep the family home in the proceedings, she could not afford the upkeep without working two jobs.

Over the course of many sessions, we explored alternative solutions for her, and the one which brought her the greatest joy was the prospect of selling her home, moving into a smaller home and having her children live with their father. Just thinking of this was uplifting to Carol, and it was constantly in her thoughts. She could taste her freedom before it was fully manifested. Such power in her resolve!

Her depression lifted, she moved forward, put her house on the market and began searching for her new home. Carol had even established the exact dollar amount of profit she wanted to earn as the result of selling her large home, after all expenses were covered. No detail was left unexplored, each one filling her with renewed faith and joy.

When her ex-husband discovered that the home was for sale, he approached his former spouse and offered her the exact amount of cash she wanted as total profit. He also volunteered to have full custody of their children, so that they could continue to live in the home in which they were raised, allowing them to remain in their same school system.

Carol was now free and clear to walk away, to live in her new home, which she had, in fact, already found. Her every creation was fulfilled! She manifested the perfect solution, and here it was! And what did she do? She turned him down! In a sudden expression of rage and hatred, Carol decided that she would never give him their home. The results of this feud turned ugly, and, as a result, he created legal circumstances that prevented her from selling the house to anyone other than himSelf.

So where is she now? Working two jobs and terribly unhappy. Is her unhappiness *his* fault, as she still claims? What was the purpose of her sudden expression of anger and hatred? Were they his fault...or her choice?

This was an interesting situation for me, for when Carol called me for advice, I was always speaking truth, and as long as I was supportive, she was happy. However, when I offered her the suggestion that she should, indeed, take her husband's offer, pointing out that it was everything she'd ever wanted, she went into a rage and I never heard from her again.

I was becoming quite frustrated with this work, since I felt unable to assist people with their issues; rather, I could only impart messages of truth that they could then accept or reject, based on their free will.

I was enjoying this aspect of my work less and less and was wondering how this would change as I mySelf continued to grow spiritually. Many clients used me as a "fortune-teller," wanting to know about marriage, jobs, etc. Why couldn't they see the greater picture of their lives? Why were so many people caught up in the day-to-day, dreaming dreams of limitation, rather than the expansion of their choices? When would people accept that they could choose to stop blaming their issues on people *outside* of themSelves and instead focus on being responsible for their own choices, thereby beginning the healing of their hearts?!

⊰ᢧᠻᡫ⊱

Hank had a lifelong dream of moving out west, and the perfect time finally arrived. No longer tied down to the formal nine-to-five routine, we were free to do our work and build our healing practice anywhere in the country. We and our daughters all chose to move to beautiful Colorado. The decision, and the move itself, occurred rather quickly, and, as sad as we were to say good-bye to dear and loving friends, we were ready for a new adventure.

One day, a few short months after our relocation, I was speaking to a friend from New Jersey, sharing with her my loneliness and the challenge we were having making new friends. Diane immediately offered to come visit to cheer me up. What a loving gesture! I accepted her offer immediately. She called soon after to tell me that Chris, her closest friend of almost twenty years, would join her. This was a surprise, for Chris and I hardly knew each other. However, I agreed, figuring that there is always great purpose when people come together.

Diane arrived early, while Chris arrived later than planned, having battled flight cancellations and other minor mishaps along the way. It was wonderful having them in our home, and soon Chris and I were talking as though we had been friends for a lifetime. She was quite relaxed and even received a "message" for us during the night, an event she had never experienced before. We all laughed, chalking it up to the energies of our home.

A few days later, Diane took an early flight home, leaving Chris in Colorado until her evening flight. I wondered what we would do together that day, since we had only really gotten to know each other that weekend. I decided to take her to the Garden of the Gods outside of Colorado Springs, a magnificent park filled with unusual outcroppings of red rocks.

We spent a wonderful day together, simply enjoying the beauty of our environment and allowing ourSelves the freedom to speak in friendship and trust. Suddenly, I perceived an energy around Chris that wished to share a message with her. When I pointed this out to her, she responded as she always had in our past work, asking me to tell her what the message was. I simply told her that she could "hear" the message herSelf, to just listen and allow it to be.

Identify the five people in your life who most profoundly impacted who you are today.

Close your eyes and thank each one, even those who taught through pain.

Then choose to energetically let them go so that you can more fully experience your life.

That next moment was to change our lives forever, for Chris suddenly began to flow the most profound and exciting truths...and she continued the flow for the rest of that day and all the way to the airport! It was a day filled with peace and joy, and the cementing of a new friendship, which was just beginning to unfold.

As time progressed, my work began to expand. I made the choice to stop the psychic work and focus all my energy on medical intuition. Clients began calling me from across the country, asking about their ailments. I was able to scan their bodies, discover the core emotional cause of their complaints and guide them along a process of healing for which they were fully responsible. I truly enjoyed assisting people in their discoveries of Self.

Meanwhile, I was in constant contact with Chris, who was beginning to change her life to adapt to this new experience which was opening up for her. I enjoyed assisting her through her spiritual growth process, an experience which always left me humble and honored.

Together, we have uncovered great truths about love, Self and God, and we support each other and all others in the expansion of this Knowing. Chris has since moved with her beautiful family to the mountains of Colorado, where we partner in our work through The Worldwide Center.

It was during this year in my partnership with Chris that my life changed profoundly. It continued to change throughout my illness. With her assistance, I chose to release energies of my childhood and allow true acceptance of my experience in this lifetime. It was an extraordinary and challenging time for me. I went through the full spectrum of emotions as I accepted total responsibility for who I was, acknowledged that I created all of my experiences, honored the perfection of my life, chose to change and release habit patterns which no longer honored me, and simply allowed mySelf to BE in each moment!

Though the words seem simple, it took almost two years of work to heal fully of the cancer I had created and come to my current state of Being. I now live in the knowing that I, in my personal perfection, have total responsibility and control of my life. I can no longer blame another for who or what I am, for I am all that I choose to be.

With these words I have shared my story. Perhaps you can relate to my personal experiences…perhaps not. No matter, for we are all the same. The most important understanding I wish to share with you is that I have healed through love. So can you.

CHAPTER FIVE

Believing in Miracles

We all are miracle workers. We each have the ability to change our lives with nothing more than a thought filled with love.

When we believe in miracles, we then create them.

Ever since I was a child, I believed in miracles. Miracles are not once-in-a-lifetime supernatural events; rather, miracles are at the root of everyday occurrences. We ourSelves are miraculous! Imagine the great Truth of who you are. Imagine the miracle of the creation of each Being: the baby who is born nine months from the moment of conception; the oak tree that was once a seed; the miracle of people flying through the air within jet planes or of voices transmitted via telephone wires; and who does not perceive the Internet as a rather miraculous feat of technology?

We live in a world filled with miracles, and yet we take them for granted. Since childhood, I was always amazed at the life around me. I watched in awe as my daughters discovered the miracles of their own hands and fingers— what baby doesn't suddenly expand their awareness to their limbs in surprise and glee? Why do we, as adults, forget to see the miracles of our world?

As one who believed in miracles, I always felt safe. It is not that I was fearless; it is simply that I knew that I would always land on my feet. When I was younger, I always felt protected by God, and so I knew that no harm would ever come to me...and it never has. But now I see the greater picture. *I created my safety simply by my belief that I am safe!*

Knowing who we are is very powerful. It is from this knowing that all miracles take place. For a miracle is simply an energy created by our choices...because we are all-powerful and limitless! Once we know that we are all-knowing, then all things become possible.

So who are we, really?

We are God!

I present this great Truth to you as a challenge, for we have all been taught that God is outside of ourSelves, a Higher Power or energetic Being, which we are separate from. Do you not believe that God is all things? Is God not the majestic mountains, the powerful oceans, the vast deserts, the endless stars in the night sky? Is God not the song of the birds, the colors of the butterflies, the strength of the mother bear defending her cubs? Can you not feel God within you as you fill with joy at the sound of a child's laughter or dance in a field filled with beautiful flowers?

All things that exist are God; so, therefore, we, too, are God! And since we are God, we have the power, as God, to create all things in our lives. And we do, whether we are aware of this truth or not. We are creating in all moments, whether we know it or not. But when we create from *love* as God, we then experience miracles!

I believe that all miracles can, and do, occur, and part of what I do in my work is to impart this belief to the hearts and minds of my clients. Cancer can be cured in a moment, once the person believes that this is so.

When we are diagnosed with life-threatening illness, we become surrounded by the grief and mourning of family and friends—and ourSelves—and it becomes difficult to acknowledge the possibility of personal growth during this experience. However, when we choose to focus on the experience as an opportunity to learn, tremendous opportunity for self-discovery is uncovered. And, as we discover the magnificence of Self with wonderment and the recognition of our power, miracles begin to happen.

I had a client, Jane*, who was directed to me following a diagnosis of an inoperable form of lung cancer. Her sister had recently died of this same ailment, so the fear in Jane's voice was palpable. The greater aspect of this diagnosis was that, because it was inoperable, it was also incurable. When Jane called, she simply requested that the work we would do energetically would make the tumor operable, so the surgeon could do the rest.

I immediately challenged her and told her that we would not do the work halfway, that she could simply and surely clear out the tumor completely! Jane was not sure she could believe that this was possible, and so I began to work with her on her belief system and self-limitation.

I worked with Jane a few times. The first session was filled with her life story, and I worked within her body to move blocks created in this lifetime, opening her up, so that she could learn to truly love herSelf. We also worked on her belief that God is separate from herSelf, so that she would be able to fully acknowledge her power. Once Jane embraced herSelf in love and acceptance, she came to recognize that the cancer was simply an experience created to teach her this very lesson, and that it was no longer necessary in her life. She chose to push away doubt and dispute the beliefs regarding the nature of her illness, and she powerfully chose to love herSelf and be empowered in her life.

Jane went to her chemotherapy sessions dressed up as though she were going to a fancy luncheon, and the doctors were always amazed at her spirit and energy. During her chemo sessions, Jane visualized armies of little soldiers marching through her body, fighting against the tumor and all stray cancer cells within her bloodstream and other organs. By her next-to-final chemo session, x-rays could not locate the offending tumor. During this session, Jane "saw" the same little armies entering her body, but when they reached the tumor itself, they found nothing but what she described as a "vast wasteland." They began a "clean-up" of the area, and Jane instinctively knew that "the grass will grow back again."

Jane chose to complete the chemo cycle, which I wholeheartedly endorsed, and she successfully became healed of her cancer. Within a period of six months after the diagnosis, this marvelous woman had turned her belief system around and embraced the miracle of her perfection.

In this instance, Jane was my teacher. Her willingness to let go of her fears regarding her illness was the true miracle, for without this choice, she would not have accomplished her goal—the full and complete release of the dis-ease within her body. I was not the healer; I was simply a facilitator, bringing Jane to the full understanding of her truth—that she is God. As God, Jane embraced her power of creation and created her renewed health.

Many people experience illness as a means of discovering their own power. Once we get past the shock of the discovery of the illness, we face many choices regarding the actions we can take in our efforts to heal. Many people who create illness choose to follow a healing path solely with a medical doctor, which is a viable option. However, if the patient gives his or her power fully to the doctor and is not an equal partner in the healing process, then the healing may be only temporary. The illness may rear its head again at some future time, because the root of the energy is still within the core of the person.

People allow the technology to do the work. They choose not to embrace their own creation of the dis-ease, and this does not honor them. Too many doctors approach a person, saying, "I will take care of this for you. Just do as I say," without bringing the *whole* person to the table. Choosing to be pro-active leads to a different experience from choosing to be disempowered...and we can freely choose to approach healing on *all* levels. More importantly, we do not need to focus on the statistics which can sink our hopes, knowing that how we experience everything in our lives is a choice and that we do not need to make choices based in fear. Instead, we can believe that anything is possible and that miracles happen every day!

When I work with a client, I approach the session, having expressed my choice about what will occur by the end of our time together. Having previously spoken with the person in order to make the appointment, I already have an idea about the issues to be worked on. A person will call me because of a pain or an imbalance in their body, and I sense the energy behind the anomaly, concentrating my energy in that region. The work I do addresses the physical body, as well as the emotional creation of the ailment.

No illness is created by accident. There is always great purpose for the experience, and this is what I help my clients discover, so that the experience of illness is no longer necessary and can be released. Each illness has a root, a core issue the person has either chosen to ignore or has concentrated an overabundance of attention upon, thus manifesting the discord.

Miracles are endless! How else could I "merge" with another's energies and feel the health or the discord within the body of that person? How do I move this invisible energy, breaking out in a sweat each time, as I force the invisible into a block and tear it free from its host? What enables me to affect the energies of selfLove so simply and quickly, working with most people during a one-and-one-half hour session, changing their lives forever? It is the miracle of my belief, transposed into their acceptance of the possibility—and once we are together in the same energy of thought, the miracle becomes their belief, and the shift occurs. They feel love in a different way—deeper, lighter, freer. And so, the healing begins.

Take the time to notice the miracles of your world. Take less for granted and pay attention to the miraculous details, the synchronicity of your life. There are no coincidences. Believe in miracles and watch them become a part of your everyday life.

What do you take for granted in your life?

List 10 miraculous things or experiences, such as the beauty of a flower, the love of a friend, etc.

We are all miracle workers. We each have the ability to change our lives with nothing more than a thought filled with love. So many people wish to change their lives but are in fear. The fear simply increases the discord they desperately want to release. If there is an aspect of your life you wish to change, it is imperative that you know what you wish to create for yourSelf, and that you desire it as an act of selfLove. It is in this energy that the miracles will take place. All healing occurs through love—love of Self—and that is the true miracle of life!

Exercise:
The Power of Why

This is a powerful way to voice positive affirmations. Acknowledging that the event has already taken place, you are allowing for its manifestation. This can be used when you wish to create an experience different from the one you are currently having. For example, if you are experiencing lack of financial abundance, "trick" your belief system by affirming that you already have abundance by saying, "Why do I have so much money?" Always use positive, pro-active word choices. The following are more examples:

Why am I resonating in perfect health?
Why am I feeling so filled with joy and peace?
Why is this day so glorious?
Why do I have enough money to pay all my bills?
Why are my children so well behaved?
Why are we having a peaceful family dinner this evening?
Why am I easily accomplishing all of my goals for today?

And so forth.

Do this exercise whenever you have a free moment—while showering, shopping, or driving to work. Simply flow with the words, have fun with it, be in joy...and be surprised at what you might hear yourSelf say!

CHAPTER SIX

Choice and Responsibility

People want their lives to change,
but they don't want to change their lives!

We have all heard that healing can be created in a moment of release, that even a person diagnosed with a life-threatening illness can suddenly and miraculously be cured! We have heard many stories of such miracles—and yet, when we ourSelves create illness within our own bodies, we are reduced to such a state of fear that it seems impossible to grow beyond that fear in order to heal. This is why so many illnesses are terminal.

Regardless of what ailment you are enduring, it is important that you recognize that this affliction is self-created. This is a difficult truth, for who would want to create a brain tumor? What person consciously chooses the experience of cancer? Who could possibly want to attract AIDS into their life?

These and other illnesses are simply the body's response to elements of one's Self-talk. That is to say that, as we diminish ourSelves from lack of selfLove, our bodies and/or our lives will reflect that choice. In addition, any accident that causes you to stop the pace of your life is also a creation of your own choosing, for how many of us really take the time to stop and smell the roses? We are not here solely to work-work-work all day long and forget the magnificence of why we have truly come to this earth! If you do not make the time to enjoy your life, be sure that, either through the creation of illness or through pain resulting from an accident, you may suddenly find yourSelf in a position which could lead you to look at your life as it is, thus giving you the opportunity to focus on changing it.

Illness is a grand opportunity for us to allow great lessons to be learned quite consciously.

When we have ignored our other, less visible or less painful attempts to hear ourSelves, illness gets our attention. The question is, how do we listen? And how do we choose to learn the lesson and ultimately heal?

I once had a dream about healing. In my dream, I was working with a young woman who had a serious illness. I had my hands over her heart chakra, front and back, and she was on her knees, rocking and moaning. There was incredible release going on, and she was moaning that she was ready to heal, that she wanted to heal. All I kept saying—no, *screaming*—over and over was, *"Do you have God? Are you with God? Can you find God? Are you not God?!"*

I awoke, still in the state I had been in within the dream, feeling deep within mySelf the understanding that, unless we make the choice to actively release all of our Self-created pain, we cannot heal. This is important to understand, for without the belief that we are all-powerful, we limit our release from pain. Without choosing to accept and *know* that we are God, we diminish ourSelves in all ways...including our ability to heal ourSelves.

I am a healing facilitator. I refuse to call mySelf a healer, as do many. It is my core belief that no one can heal another, that, whether we know it or not, we are *all* healers, for we *each* have the power, as God, to heal ourSelves, body, mind and soul. Just as there is no such thing as a magic pill, there is no magic person who can heal *you*, except your*Self!*

In my work, I have witnessed many people making the choice to release painful energies, in the process of letting go of the dis-eases manifested by their bodies. It is sometimes quite difficult to watch someone suddenly recognize a truth that has long been dormant, a truth so vile to that person that it created inner turmoil at the cellular level of the body, thereby creating the dysfunction of the body's natural experience. However, once this truth is recognized and released in its entirety, the ailment more easily diminishes and disappears. Of course, it is equally vital that new paradigms be created in the person's life, in order not to recreate the ailment!

It is very difficult to accept that we have chosen to bring health challenges into our lives. But it is important to remember that, in every moment, we have free will. Whatever we bring into our lives as thought, we create. Likewise, if we have an experience we do not enjoy, we can learn from this creation and, through new thoughts, bring forth different creations!

Remember, as God, all things exist without judgment. There is no right or wrong in the eyes of God—in *our* eyes! There is simply experience. What experiences are you choosing in this lifetime? Illness is not a *negative* creation, just one filled with challenge and, ultimately, the opportunity for growth and knowledge.

An important lesson for each of us to learn in this lifetime is that we are here to experience complete freedom of choice. This may sound simple, but it goes far deeper than we imagine at first glance. Choice occurs in each and every moment of our lives! Every word expressed, each emotion felt, all thoughts from within—these are of our own choosing, and they result in the physical expression of the world around us.

No one is responsible for the anger you feel towards another except *you*, regardless of the action taken by the other person who provoked this reaction *from* you! In any given moment, you may choose to hold on to this anger, or you may more healthfully choose to release it. The choice is totally yours. The other person's behavior towards you is simply an opportunity for change and growth within yourSelf!

And, taking this one step further, you are also responsible for the results created by your choices. If you respond to someone in anger and speak with dishonoring words to or about that person, this behavior is *your* choice, and *you* become responsible for this action. No one *made* you take this path of action; you *chose it.*

Choice and responsibility go hand in hand. We have all, at one time or another, blamed others for how we feel, thereby choosing to place responsibility for our own actions upon another. How ludicrous! If we have an argument with our spouse, throughout the interaction we always have the choice to pull back into silence and release (not suppress!) the anger. We are not here to change each other; we are here to experience ourSelves, and if we are unhappy with a circumstance of our lives, we can choose to change it.

We can choose to discover how to love ourSelves by looking carefully at how we treat ourSelves. How do you speak about yourSelf? Do you let people know how well you do things or how wonderful you are, or do you diminish yourSelf with your words and thoughts?

SelfLove is not only how you choose to treat yourSelf, it is also how you choose to think of yourSelf. I once asked a client if she loved herSelf, and she told me that she did, indeed, for, after all, she had a manicure every week and a monthly massage. Is this selfLove? Yes. But she also told me that she had gained some weight and looked horrible, and that her hair had lost its luster, and she looked terrible in all ways. Are these words of selfLove?

I am not telling you to lie to yourSelf. But I am showing you that you have a choice to change your experience from one of pain to one of selfLove. If you are unhappy with your weight, for instance, there is much that can be done about it, and you must take responsibility for your choices. If you are unhappy with your hair, take responsibility and seek the help of a professional hairdresser. If you choose to keep telling yourSelf—and your body—that you look terrible, what happens is that you will create the look with the thought that this is so. It will not change unless you see yourSelf in a loving, wonderful way, and make the choice of changing how you look. Take responsibility for the thoughts and actions that create your life as you know it to be, and allow new choices to change your personal life experience!

I have a client, Sabrina*, who is quite familiar with the spiritual/new age vocabulary of our times. She has worked with a number of healers on the same issues. Time and again, Sabrina has been abandoned—by her parents, a sibling, her caregiver growing up, assorted lovers and her husband. Sabrina holds on to this powerful abandonment energy by talking about it endlessly. She has a young child who reflects her fears of abandonment, and there is a powerful part of Sabrina that is creating her own possible abandonment of this child, since she is considering allowing his father full custody.

I do not judge her choices. I simply move into her core truth, to determine whether her creation is the result of her own sense of limitation or if it is indeed an act that will serve the highest good of all involved.

Sabrina does not take responsibility for her choices; she simply blames her actions on her experiences from childhood. Because she is not choosing to fully love herSelf, she focuses her energy on all that has *not* been in her life, rather than what is. She whines about her inability to stay in one place for very long, or to share energy for long with any one person, including her child. She claims to love herSelf and uses this language of selfLove as her excuse to move into her "freedom" (i.e. "It's because I love mySelf that I have to leave..." etc.).

This would be true only if she *were* choosing in selfLove, but she is not. A choice made in selfLove would bring Sabrina peace. She is not at peace with her life, and she is always looking for something else to do or somewhere else to go. In addition, Sabrina still struggles with the pain of abandonment and is comfortable in this pain. She has not yet taken the responsibility of letting it go and moving beyond it. Therefore, her choices are not honoring herSelf or anyone else around her. Until then, Sabrina will continue to struggle emotionally, as she has for most of her life.

There are circumstances of life which are quite challenging and, for some, difficult to accept. Many of my clients were victims of child abuse and have carried this victimization into their adulthood. Understand that, while the emotional and physical pain of such trauma is to be honored, each person who survives such a childhood always has the choice of how they wish to live the rest of their lives.

Embracing pain is a challenging undertaking, but it can be done. Many have created wonderful lives following years of childhood abuse. It takes great courage and work. It takes honesty and choice. It takes the willingness to accept responsibility for *this* moment of their lives, by honoring and releasing the years of trauma and pain.

The outcome of the childhood abuse is the core of the issue: Will the abused choose a life of endless pain and self-recrimination? Or will the abused overcome the horrors of childhood and powerfully create a full and vital life filled with love and understanding?

Recognize that, with choice, comes responsibility! One path is to hold on to the pain for an entire lifetime, using it as an excuse to create a world where love and trust are lacking. It is a different choice to claim responsibility for one's own life and instead to release these same horrors. The difference here is how one will choose to experience life and living—in pain or joy, fear or peace. Ultimately, the learning is that *all* choices are equal.

And what of the child who dies in youth due to a debilitating illness, such as leukemia or a brain tumor? Is this a choice? Of course, it is. This little being has chosen this experience as an aspect of life and living. The soul of this child chose this experience prior to birth, not only for the experience itself, but to allow a greater experience for those who share his or her short life, thus allowing each person involved the perfect opportunity for growth from this powerful choice.

The child comes as a great teacher, providing those who are left behind with the opportunity for acceptance, change and understanding. The grief cannot be denied, but these others will either continue or stop in the moment of the transition, each choice being an opportunity to come to terms with life. It becomes the choice of each person involved in this experience whether or not they will choose an expansion of life from this event.

In order to heal, love should be expressed and shared—with Self and others. Release can be experienced. And a great understanding that life is eternal can be the result. The child leaves behind a broken body, but the soul's experience becomes much more glorious as the result of this choice.

Accepting full responsibility for your life enables you to choose more powerfully all that you wish to experience. Rather than seeking to lay blame for the difficulties you endure, you can pro-actively take on the responsibility for your choices and then change your life by making new choices.

An abused wife can always make the choice to leave her abusive husband; yet, how many times will she blame her choice to stay on lack of money, or the children, or an endless litany of excuses? The victim is not to be blamed for the abuse, but once she recognizes her patterns of self-limitation, she can be empowered to take control of her life. By giving away her power to her husband or to the limitations of her life (which she herSelf created!), she remains in *self-created* bondage that will never release her unless she chooses to free herSelf from the notion that she is "stuck." We are *never* stuck. We are *always* free. We have the freedom to choose to take our personal power and move into the reality we wish to experience!

All things are possible. We limit ourSelves simply because of ideas we embrace—ideas taught to us by those outside ourSelves and ones we choose to hold onto. Some of these teachings come from those we most trust—our families, our teachers, our religious leaders, our government. What we forget to do is listen to the little voice we each carry within our hearts, the voice of our true connection, the God that we are! As we learn to listen to our inner voice, we free ourSelves to live. As we see our world through the eyes of our greatness, we never again have to deal with limitation. As we allow our actions to be the expression of our selfLove, we then have the ability to easily understand our personal challenges...and overcome them. As we allow our "knowing" to guide us, then we are truly upon the path of empowerment.

᳁᳁᳁

People want their lives to change, but they don't want to change their lives!

We each have the power to heal, and healing is a choice. My husband Hank once had a client who contacted him about using his method of healing with her, since she had been told it was quite powerful. This woman was always quite ill but never with anything life-threatening. She was seeking to change her life experience of illness to one of wellness and needed assistance.

A few days after working with her, Hank received a frantic telephone call from this same client, asking him if they could "reverse" this healing because it had worked too well! She *wanted* to be ill, because, in illness, she received much more attention from her husband than she did in wellness.

In a different example, Shari* was living a healthy, "normal" life. She was unhappy in some aspects, and chose to go to a variety of healers, both medical (psychologists) and non-medical (alternative spiritual guides), in order to experience greater joy. During her many sessions, it was discovered that she had been severely sexually abused as a child. Although Shari had no conscious memory of the abuse, once she had this information, her mental condition deteriorated so dramatically that she was unable to get out of bed and face each day. This was her situation when she contacted me.

I was quite firm with Shari, challenging her and teaching her that her life choice in *this* moment was fully her responsibility. Unlike most around her, I chose not to coddle her choice of "being the victim;" rather, I told her it was time to get up and face the world in the *now* of her life and release what had been. After all, she truly had no memory of anything violent, only the imprint of thought brought forth by another—and could there not be error here?

Shari was gaining great benefit through her choice to create mental illness and was unwilling to take responsibility. She would speak only of the horrible pain she had endured as a child, refusing to live in this moment of her life, choosing instead to hold on to the emotional paralysis created by these memories. I chose not to work with Shari as a client until she was willing to acknowledge her choices, offering my services when she chose to recognize her power to choose differently.

Illness is a choice, although generally one we are not aware of having made. Much attention is gained when one is weak and unable to be in perfect health. As a parent, I mySelf gave my children undivided attention and unusual devotion during times when they were ill. What I recognized was that they also needed such attention when they were healthy, in order to create balance and not allow them to seek love through illness.

My own grandmother would never admit to being in good health, because she received much more attention from family members by always complaining of this health issue or that pain. Her energy ultimately created a situation of true illness, which perhaps would have been avoided, had she chosen to joyously live in the perfection of her true healthy state.

Imagine what your life would be like if you could have everything you want—health, wealth, happiness and peace. Why are so many people so sure that they can never achieve all these things and more? What has created this limitation of expectation? If you were told that, in a single moment, you could change your life and have all that you desire, how far would you go to

Identify one thing you have always wanted to experience in your life. It could be a true friend, visiting an exotic place, etc.

Write down what choices you have to make to create this new reality. What behaviors do you need to change, and are you willing to do so?

make that choice? What are you willing to change, or perhaps give up, or even embrace, in order to achieve your every dream?

Although the question sounds simple enough, if you were to take a moment and analyze your choices, how far would you go in order to create change in your life? Would you quit your job if you were asked to do so, in order to create profound healing in your life? Would you divorce your spouse if this choice would bring you freedom and happiness? Would you change your diet? Would you move from your current home into another?

These questions are not being asked lightly, for, in many instances, I have made such suggestions to my clients. To what degree of commitment are they willing to partner with me in their healing? How far are they willing to go to create change in their lives and heal their hearts?

When I work with my clients, I make them responsible for their own healing. I am always surprised when I discover at a later date that the homework they were given remained undone. Perhaps they were advised to change their diet in order to more fully honor their body, or perhaps I suggested they drink much more water, or do simple breathing exercises. If any of my clients refuse to embrace change by choice, I can no longer assist them, for they are not taking on the required responsibility for themSelves. Remember, they are their own healers, and, as such, they have the responsibility of doing what it takes to heal! I simply aid them in the facilitation of this choice, but ultimately *they* are responsible!

I had a client, Sylvia*, who called me because she was suffering from a chronic pain in her foot. Due to this pain, Sylvia had difficulty walking and had already gone to a medical doctor, who had advised her to keep off the foot for a few days. Sylvia had ignored this advice and, naturally, the foot did not heal. When she called me, we went through the entire healing experience together, discovering that the pain in her foot was energetically due, in part, to her feeling "stuck," an inability to move forward in her life, along with a weight issue which added stress to the physical body. I did energy work on her foot, and Sylvia was able to feel the energy, much to her surprise and delight. Like the doctor, I advised her to remain off the foot for a couple of days.

When Sylvia contacted me a couple of weeks later, she told me her foot was still not healed, but sheepishly admitted that she had continued walking on it, even after our work, and was now on crutches. Where was Sylvia's responsibility towards her own healing? What choices was she making, and why was she choosing to dishonor her body?

When we love ourSelves, we allow for self-healing. In selfLove, we willingly take the actions needed to create the life we want. When experiencing selfLove, we live more peacefully and harmoniously with Self and others, choosing and calling forth positive experiences in our lives. We are always perfect in every state of Being, but we experience great joy when we make choices of selfLove.

SelfLove is the choice to accept and honor all aspects of Self as magnificent...and never to diminish, even for a moment, the perfection of who you are.

We always have the choice of reclaiming our power. Our creations are the result of thoughts, words and choice through actions. Mindful creation is the active expression of knowing who you are and, from this knowing, experiencing your power. As you experience self-empowerment, you can mindfully allow your reality to unfold, and you do so from acknowledging your magnificence. When you choose to experience selfLove, your creations will manifest the joy that you are.

When we choose from mindful thought, we become much more aware of the neglectful choices we make out of habit. For example, if you are dealing with a weight issue and wish to shed a few pounds, you can choose to become aware of your daily eating habits. You can choose to be responsible for your choices and reach for an apple rather than a cookie, drink extra glasses of water rather than the usual soda, eat a large salad rather than a bowl of pasta. You can choose to climb the stairs rather than take the elevator, but to do so, you need to choose to overcome a habit pattern created by years of simply taking the elevator. In other words, through choice and self-empowerment, you will override habit and create a new paradigm, in order to choose a new experience.

When we make choices based upon what has always been done before, we are reacting to our environment without thought. We are allowing old patterns to govern us, rather than taking hold of our ability to choose differently each time. And in either case, we are responsible for the action, for it was our choice.

As we choose to willingly do the *work* that creates change in our lives, changes occur. It is so simple, yet it does take effort! With nothing more than a thought, we can change our lives, for our thoughts create shifts in energy. But we must also follow that thought with action, and from this action, we put forth our true choice about shifting into this new experience! Your body will not drink additionally-needed water unless you mindfully choose to reach for the glass, fill it with water and drink it. And if drinking more water is what it takes to help you release toxins from your body and bring you to greater health, should it be very difficult to do so? Surprisingly, a great many of my clients complain about how hard it is to drink more water every day. And this complaining creates an energy of even greater difficulty, thus creating greater blocks to success. A simple act of drinking more water to improve health becomes a task they refuse to responsibly embrace...and this becomes their choice, ultimately blocking their ability to heal.

When we choose to take responsibility through our thoughts and actions, allowing this choice to become a true motivating factor towards change, we are flowing in selfLove. *Loving ourSelves enough to take action that honors us ultimately allows us to experience our joy and the recognition that we are perfect, resulting in total healing.*

Once we experience our perfection by loving ourSelves, we move into the energy flow of creating a balanced body and total health. We can choose to release obstacles that are self-created and beliefs that we embrace that have been introduced to us via our families, our schools, our churches and our governments. We are all born perfect, and we can choose to experience our perfection in each moment of our lives!

Exercises:

Honoring Your Choices

1. Write a paragraph on each of the three most important choices you ever made in your life that honored you in joy. Discuss why these choices were important.

2. Repeat one hundred times the words "I love me because I *chose* (Choice #1, #2 & #3) in my life."

3. Repeat one hundred times the words "I love me because I *choose* (Choice #1, #2 & #3) in my life."

CHAPTER SEVEN

Growth through Trauma

For most of us, it is easy to blame childhood circumstances when we face habit patterns that do not honor the adult that we are.

Trauma is created by a wide range of life situations. When one considers trauma, it is most usually thought of in terms of sexual abuse or rape. Yet, for many, the body responds to the death of a child or a spouse as though it were traumatized. For others, a severe or debilitating accident or illness creates their body's trauma. Each of these and other traumas are opportunities for growth and expansion; however, each individual should be treated carefully. No two people are the same, and each person deserves the respect of not being treated generically.

Trauma creates profound energetic shifts within a person's body, and to avoid physical repercussions in later years, the root of this energy must be released. Traditional therapies work to a degree, but more than the trauma itself should be acknowledged; rather, all aspects of the person—body, mind and spirit—should be involved, in order to promote total healing.

Victims of severe sexual abuse have an unusually difficult time releasing energies of rage, creating within their bodies and spirits a sense of defeat and an inability to move into new creations with ease. Traditional therapies have them review the events of the abuse, reopening chapters of horror, which serve to hold time in limbo, rather than exploring new avenues to build upon in the creation of their glorious future. Many clients have told me that they have released their rage at their abuser; yet, I always sensed energies which were still waiting in hiding, building walls and blocks that would come to the surface in a moment, should a memory be suddenly triggered.

Letting go and releasing the experience of pain and the emotions toward the abuser are powerful choices. However, to be most effective, these choices should be based on more than words and conscious thought. The rage can be replaced with love—love of Self and love of the other. It is important to acknowledge the rage, but also to choose to experience love and peace through acceptance of what was. Although victims of abuse focus on trying to forgive their abusers (as well as themSelves), forgiveness carries judgment, not acceptance. Acceptance and love are what is needed to release the pain from the heart of the victim.

In most cases, it takes many years for victims of childhood sexual abuse to release the energies of fear and rage, and it can take just as long for the victim of a violent rape. No trauma is greater or lesser than another, though many of these victims feel that their trauma is worse than another's. It is unnecessary to compare; the psyche is stronger or weaker in different individuals, and the pain and horror of any form of abuse should be addressed with equal compassion and love.

To use New Age jargon, as do many alternative therapists and healers, and discuss the fact that the abuse was a "soul contract" does not honor the person who was the victim of the torment. The explanation that this was a soul choice for soul growth does not remove the pain and anguish that have been experienced. Not only does it do little to change the reality of living in this physical body in this moment of time, but this is usually the last thing the victim wants to hear. They are powerfully dealing with the memories, the trauma and the shame of the physical experience.

I have had a number of clients who were horrendously sexually abused by their parents. Both parents are always involved, for, although one may be the perpetrator, the other is the enabler. One of these clients suffered from multiple personality disorder as a result; another became a homeless street person before rebuilding her life; and others suffered from varying degrees of dissociative personality disorders. I have listened to stories which were true nightmares, and yet, as these clients shared their tales of horror, I maintained an energy of compassion, love and acceptance. I honor these people for their courage in experiencing this trauma and overcoming it as they have. It has taken them much time and energy, challenging their very day-to-day existence. We should never belittle the fears created by such trauma. We should never lay blame on the rape victim. We can choose to look beyond the physical and come to an understanding of the issues at play, but always within the realm of acceptance and compassion.

Children of abuse make basic choices as the result of the years of torture they endure. It sometimes takes a lifetime to release the effects of the abuse. Illness is created, both mental and physical, when one's own safety is so profoundly challenged by the actions of another. And when children are the victims, their helplessness is even greater. But these abused children grow up, and in adult bodies they often either choose powerless existences or create a repetition of abuse upon another generation of innocent children.

Of the clients I have worked with who are survivors of childhood sexual abuse, no two needed the same energies in their healing. There is no one pathway towards success along this avenue, for each person carries his or her own blueprint of energy, allowing for his or her own personal survival and recovery.

Using either yourself or someone you know who has experienced trauma, identify three powerful habit patterns that resulted from the trauma. Think about what would need to change to establish new patterns of behavior.

One person with multiple personalities whom I worked with was Abigail*. For years, while on her traditional healing path, she had been a spiritual seeker, so when she and I came together to further her healing, she was truly well-read and knowledgeable, having created for herSelf a powerful relationship with God. She always kept her image of God as being *outside* of herSelf. Perhaps this was because there were so many aspects of personalities already within her that this was less complicated for her mind to deal with. However, her lack of self-worth, even in her recovery, kept her from knowing her power.

Abigail felt quite comfortable allowing the multiple personalities to run her life, and although she always spoke of totally merging, her fear was greater than her desire. With her multiple personalities, she never had to be accountable for her actions or choices; rather, she maintained the drama of being a victim of these very personalities who had been created to protect her.

While working with a few of these clients, a challenging concept occurred to me. I discovered that victims of childhood trauma are generally of above-average intelligence, regardless of their levels of education. This intelligence was indeed key to their survival. Many years had passed since their abuse and, during much of this time, they admirably underwent great healing. Most had created lives that appeared totally normal to the outside world and, since they were individuals on their own personal pathways, some were further along in their freedom than others. Some were stuck in old patterns and attempted to manipulate the conversation during our session, rather than dealing with a challenging truth I would present to them. In their day-to-day experiences, many successfully used this tool, since they were able to handle the art of manipulation so intelligently.

In a large number of instances, I observed that, during a moment of challenge and responsibility, there would be a shift of "personalities" that would spring forth in order to prevent the core personality from facing choices which would bring great change to that person's lifestyle. It was simply a continuation of an instinctual survival mechanism, which had honored them during their years of trauma but had yet to be released. This release is important in order to bring about profound healing.

For most of us, it is easy to blame childhood circumstances when we face habit patterns that do not honor the adult that we are. We can be in our forties or fifties and still talk about how life was at "home" when we were children, as though this is an acceptable excuse for challenging adult behavior. We can all choose to release this way of avoiding true responsibility for our actions. We live each moment in the *present*, the *now* of our lives! We have total freedom to let go of the past and experience the newness of each moment's creation! This does not mean that we will forget that which was; rather, we have the power to put what *was* in its place and know that, in each moment, we are creating each experience we move into, the *is* that we are, living in the *now!*

Alice* is a woman who lost a child over a year ago. This traumatic experience paralyzed her, even though the twin of this lost child survived and there was another, older sibling. Alice experienced such grief that she was barely able to nurture her remaining two beautiful children, and her marriage was threatened. It was as though, in Alice's life, time stood still. What a fascinating creation!

Alice was unable and unwilling to move into the work that was proposed to her. She refused to accept the notion that there was important purpose in this life experience, and that the child who left did so in great love at a soul level, allowing Alice powerful growth in this lifetime. Alice was, in fact, holding on so tightly to this lost child that she was creating harm to herSelf, to this child and to the rest of her family. She was unwilling to release her grief. This was pure choice on her part, for she was totally capable of doing so, as we all are, but only by choosing to be pro-active in her life. She would have honored herSelf by embracing her grief fully, thus allowing the energies to flow through each stage of release, and then embracing the present moment of her Being. But in her mind, Alice was stuck in one moment—the moment of the death of this child—and therefore felt paralyzed, unable to allow life to move forward. Ultimately, without healing, Alice would be on the road to creating illness in her Being, both physically and mentally. And her living children would face their own issues in adulthood, which they could then choose to release.

Although we are responsible for no one other than ourSelves, our actions do profoundly affect those around us. To what degree is of their own choosing, and all interactions are of great purpose, leading towards spiritual growth and human development. The experiences of trauma and abuse are among life's many challenges, and the choice to heal in love is ultimately the greatest and most powerful gift one can give oneSelf.

Exercise:
Releasing Trauma

1. Choose a person with whom you have experienced trauma or a dramatic encounter.

   a) Write a letter to this person, thanking him or her for coming into your life as your teacher, and acknowledging what you learned during the shared experience of pain.

   b) Take the time to fully reveal to yourSelf the aspects of the experience that made you stronger, then let him or her go as you honor what you learned.

2. You can choose to keep the letter, mail it, throw it away or burn it. But choose that, once the letter is written, you have accepted and released the experience as a powerful expression of selfLove.

CHAPTER EIGHT

Letting Go—Living in Freedom

We do not let anything go unless we embrace it with love.

There is a generally accepted belief that one cannot heal if the path to forgiveness has not been chosen—forgiveness of others, forgiveness of Self. We harbor within our hearts much energy which we embrace from the actions of others, and although we may mindfully choose to release these energies, we believe that the release is not complete without total and unconditional forgiveness.

Seeking forgiveness, though, is the result of one's personal judgment—that another's experience or choice is "less acceptable" or "unworthy," compared to a different choice or experience. All choices are equal—just different. Forgiveness does not allow healing; rather, it shifts the energy of pain from anger to denial. It is not with forgiveness that we free ourSelves from pain. We free ourSelves with unconditional acceptance and love.

We can learn to let go of all that has been and allow each experience to simply be a life experience which we have called forth in order to learn. It is important to choose the freedom that comes from letting go—of memories, of painful feelings held onto for years, and even of actions by others around us. We can choose to allow each person his or her choice to act, to speak, to not love themSelves in any way they choose, so that we are then choosing to fly free of that same energy by simply putting it to rest.

We do not let anything go unless we embrace it with love. By doing so, we acknowledge and honor our choice to experience and learn from it. Once we have done so, our choices can be released.

Choosing to experience freedom means that we are willing to go within the heart of our own Being to determine the great truth of our personal experiences. We can choose to look upon the circumstances of our lives and release issues which we perceive as having denied us our freedom. We can choose to be in non-judgment and allow the experiences to simply be that...and thus release ourSelves from the emotions which leave us frozen in time.

In circumstances of severe abuse in childhood, the now-grown adult can choose to recognize that the experience is complete, that time has progressed and that, as an adult embracing choice and free will, he or she can release the vestiges of energies created by the trauma. This statement is simplistic, for tremendous work may need to be done to come to peace within the present moment. However, we do have the ability to overcome all perceived obstacles in our lives, if we choose to do so in selfLove. To honor the choice to learn through abuse is a giant step towards healing. More importantly, once we choose to allow the abuser his or her choices of pain, it is easier to release our own shame and guilt, since we recognize that accepting the other calls forth deeper acceptance of Self.

In working with survivors of childhood abuse, I recognize the challenge of choosing to let go. Some clients even use the words, but the body still reflects deep-seated rage which has yet to be released. These victims are simply that—victims of years of horrors which were still impacting their present lives—but they must recognize that now they are victimizing themSelves. Most, by holding on to the memories of pain, fear and anger, had become their own abusers in adulthood. I assist them in working towards coming to the understanding that they can choose to free themSelves— not of the abuse, but of the hatred they still hold at the center of their Being.

In everyday circumstances of life and living, we perceive insults thrust upon us by others. These are truly only perceptions, for we choose to perceive the words or actions as insulting and we can just as easily choose not to. So many friendships and family relationships are challenged by simple moments of miscommunication or action. The anger and pain that one chooses in reaction harbors discord within the physical body of each party involved. The end of a friendship is akin to the death of a friend. The animosity between family members often creates a lifetime of separation and grief.

Freedom begins with the active choice of accepting that all that was experienced was in its perfection, and continues with the choice to let go of the past and experience Now.

As we look back upon the experiences we have brought into our lives, we can choose to acknowledge that we have created these experiences in order to learn and to change. There are no accidents, just as there are no coincidences. Each and every interaction serves great purpose. It offers us the opportunity to acknowledge our power to choose differently.

Our most painful experiences are rooted in a powerful lack of selfLove, offering us great opportunity to recognize old patterns and choose new ones in selfLove. Challenging interactions shared between people offer great opportunities to release old patterns of behavior, learn about our hearts and let go of limitation, so we can experience all that we are. Once these challenging interactions are played out, we have the choice of either harboring the pain of the conflict in our hearts, which can affect us in challenging ways, or of releasing the energies of the experience and allowing ourSelves greater freedom.

We cannot experience our freedom as long as we hold energies of pain with any other human Being. Freedom is an experience of Self without limitation; to experience freedom, we have to make the choice to embrace and accept all relationships. This does not mean that we will be friends with all people or all family members. What it *does* mean, however, is that we can allow each person his or her own idiosyncrasies, without judgment and, in many cases, without unnecessary interactions with them, as long as we harbor no ill will towards them because of who they choose to be and how they choose to express themSelves in this lifetime.

As a child, Michael* was sexually abused by his mother. His father, a traveling salesman, was away from home when these episodes occurred and was unaware of this abuse. Interestingly, when Michael's father was at home, he was a very harsh and demanding man, and the entire family lived in fear of his outbursts and tirades.

Michael grew up to be quite promiscuous and struggled with alcoholism for most of his life. When sharing his story with me, he calmly spoke of the sexual abuse, but his rage grew when he discussed his father. Michael had transmuted the anger of his abuse to the wrong parent, choosing to focus more heavily upon his fear of his father's rages, rather than emotionally touching upon the feelings he struggled with regarding his mother's abusiveness.

Michael truly hated his father and made no bones about it. In contrast, he called his mother a saint and held her on a pedestal, crying when he told me of her passing. Michael refused to discuss accepting his father; nor would he see the need to release his mother. I was able to assist him in recognizing his innocence as a child and his lack of responsibility for the confusion the abuse brought to his young mind, but I knew that Michael would not experience the freedom of release until he willingly acknowledged and accepted, in his heart, the truth about his youth.

We are yearning to be free—free of the pain and unworthiness we feel. We will never experience total freedom as long as we choose to hold on to energies which do not honor us. We can, instead, choose to honor, without judgment, any and all aspects of our lives and all choices we have made, so that we can accept their perfection. We can choose to release the energies created by others' actions toward us, both real and perceived, because we call forth each experience in order for all to learn, and we can choose to honor our souls for leading us along pathways for growth.

Health challenges can be easily released by choosing to experience total freedom—for Self and for All. When I work with people to release core issues of rage, they face the choice of letting go of all that has been. We each can think of people in our lives who have created disharmony in some way, but we can also remember that holding on to the energies of the disharmony is of our own choosing. The disharmony can become the root of an imbalance in mind, body or spirit and will truly fester with time. Releasing the disharmony is a path towards freedom, allowing all aspects of Being to resonate in total health and well-being.

Choose freedom. Take a powerful step for your own health and allow your heart to let go of anger which does not honor you. Honor yourSelf and others in your life, and choose always to interact with acceptance. When angered, allow the emotion to simply wash through you; accept it and honor it, then let it go. We have the power to make new choices in all moments, each choice creating an experience of pain...or joy. Acknowledge the perceived "flaws" of Self and others, and recognize that there is always perfection. Each moment is an opportunity to learn. Make the most of it, and heal by choosing freedom in your heart.

Exercises:
Learning from Your Pain

1. List the major incidents of your life.

2. Examine your feelings regarding these major incidents that you are holding inside yourSelf.
   a) Discuss how each incident challenged you.
   b) What did you learn from each incident?
   c) How did each incident change you?
   d) How will your life change once you release the emotions attached to each incident?

3. Ask yourSelf if you are willing to give up the badge of victimhood that comes with holding on to pain. How will you talk and act differently if you give up the pain?

CHAPTER NINE

Self-Empowerment, The Path to Healing

*In order to heal pain in our hearts and bodies, we must choose to heal
by letting go of that which sustains the pain and fear.*

Generally, a person who is facing a physical, mental or emotional challenge feels powerless. During challenging experiences, we are suddenly— and importantly—faced with the need to acknowledge our power.

Powerlessness is, in most instances, rooted in childhood. Parents, sometimes unwittingly, clip the wings of their children simply by not permitting them the freedom to fly. In many cases, these wings never rejuvenate, even after these children grow into adulthood, because the ties to the powerful parent remain quite strong. A co-dependency is established, and the adult child is fearful of creating emotional stirrings in the heart of the parent. Interestingly, the parent is equally powerless and uses the emotions of the children to feel more powerful. The struggle is due to pain. Although there is shared love between the family members, it is limited, simply because life itself is limited within the walls of powerlessness.

I have had the honor of working with many members of a single family, each struggling with different challenges: depression, chronic fatigue syndrome, colitis, fear of success. The center of this family was a dominant mother, who viewed herSelf as a loving person whose life revolved around her adult children. This mother truly loved her children as well as she was able to, unaware that her love was limited...and limiting. Her children

Look critically at how you relate to your parents and siblings.

Do you speak openly and honestly? Do you choose to remain silent and separate from them?

Now look at why you make these choices.

Do you feel unaccepted?

Develop a list of choices you could make to change this relationship, and choose to act on them.

never moved too far from their family home, even in marriage, and the extended family spent much time together. Conversations were limited, in order to maintain harmony and to avoid upsetting the mother, who had episodes of hysteria when she felt betrayed or attacked, even when this wasn't the case.

Although this family prided itself on its closeness, none of the family members were in their truth, for they were always being careful about what they said or did. Symptoms of illness or stress began to surface, the product of holding back and limiting full expression. By their own choosing, the family members were powerless in their individual lives. Even the mother was powerless—hence, the episodes of hysteria, created in an effort to control her world.

In another family with a similar scenario, the adult children chose to disassociate from their mother emotionally. Again, the children lived nearby, but, interestingly, the family rarely came together except on major holidays, and there was always great tension at these gatherings. This mother, in contrast to the example above, was in such powerlessness that her effort to control her family was expressed through self-denial. She always complained about how difficult her life was and how much she had sacrificed for her children. She was always demanding that her children do time-consuming tasks for her, because she "couldn't" do them for herSelf, and they "owed" her so much because of her sacrifices. The result was that communication between parent and child, or between the siblings, became limited.

Although, in this case, it may appear that each person made a choice to honor him/herSelf by creating this separation, in truth, the emotional energies were still creating discord within the individuals. The wings were still broken on these baby birds.

No one was truly willing to confront the issues at play, and the drama continued, simply because their fear of expressing the truth appeared to be more powerful than the ultimate outcome. It would be challenging for these adult children to face their mother with the truth that they no longer had joy being "forced" to deal with her personal limitations, but this sharing, with open hearts, could bring all of them, including their mother, freedom.

Sherry* was a woman who had left home at an early age, running away from an abusive childhood. When we met, she was in her forties and still running. She'd had a lifetime of embracing and conquering alcoholism and drug addiction and was finally choosing to let go. Sherry had difficulty reclaiming her power. She felt unworthy, because of issues from years ago. Twelve years of therapy had been of great help, but there was a strong dependency transferred to her therapist, rooted in her feelings of powerlessness.

Sherry chose to hold on to memories, rather than to create a life based in freedom. She punished herSelf with her self-deprecation and blamed the ills of her choices on her childhood. Sherry had to choose to embrace her full responsibility for Self before she could embrace her power.

She felt isolated emotionally from the world, and it was important that she learn to see herSelf in all her magnificence. She had already enjoyed glimpses of her power, but sabotaged herSelf when things went too well for her for too long. She did not feel worthy to be as successful as she has the potential to become, and is still in the process of simply allowing the past to disappear from her present reality.

Another client, Judy*, came to me with symptoms of Multiple Sclerosis (MS), although I intuitively knew that this was not her true situation. The symptoms were primarily muscle weakness in her arms and legs, and, through her fear, two things became apparent: first, her belief that she had MS had the potential to *create* this illness; and second, her weakness was simply a manifestation of her lack of power and selfLove.

Judy never married. Instead, she was married to a family she was devoted to, but who did not honor her in return. Judy's devotion to her mother was based in guilt over her father's death years earlier, and her sense of obligation to her mother prevented Judy from ever freeing herSelf from her role as her mother's caregiver. Her mother played into this drama by always being needy; she was an otherwise healthy woman, who chose to use her children to do everything she needed to have done. Although other relatives would offer their services, Judy's mother believed that it was her children's duty to take care of her, and so she would not permit any assistance from someone else.

To complicate this situation, Judy's siblings refused to participate in this family drama, leaving the majority of the obligation on Judy's shoulders. Judy's rage was never focused towards her mother, who embodied the energy thwarting Judy's freedom. Instead, she felt great anger towards her siblings for abandoning her. She was unwilling to let go of her core belief that she was right and her siblings wrong. Also, Judy would never take a much-needed vacation, claiming that she could not leave her mother, even though I presented to her that this was her choice, and that her mother would survive the separation. And finally, Judy kept a powerful focus upon her ailment, actually looking for symptoms when they were absent.

Judy was creating illness in order to receive the same attention she paid to her mother. Deep within her heart, Judy wanted to be taken care of and, by creating this illness, she was seeking to change roles within her family so that she would no longer be the caregiver. Healthier options are always available through acts of selfLove and self-empowerment. That is when we fully recognize that we cannot be manipulated in our lives unless we, at some level, give permission to be.

In order to heal pain in our hearts and bodies, we must choose to heal by letting go of that which sustains the pain and fear. As we let go of what no longer serves us in joy, we can then choose to embrace new paradigms, knowing that we have the ability to achieve freedom simply by creating new pathways.

So many spiritual seekers believe that the path must be difficult or challenging. What a powerful creation! Would you rather struggle to be free, or would you rather simply allow freedom to permeate your life easily and quickly? Who is to say that this latter choice cannot be possible? *It is important to always remember who you are!*

To be in our power is to accept the magnificence of who we are. We are God. So simple, so true. All that exists is God. As we accept that we are truly powerful, then we can allow this knowledge to create, with joy, the manifestation of our glorious lives! A person who is filled with fear will always create fearful circumstances in their lives. A person aware of his or her personal joy will continue along this path of joy, simply by recognizing it. All thoughts have the power to create! Watch your words, your thoughts and your actions, for they are all-powerful.

How do we experience self-empowerment? Allow this concept to become your reality simply by exploring the possibilities! Put forth a simple intention in total knowing. You must be *certain* of that thought...that it will be. *Certainty is the knowing, without doubt, that your creation is your reality.*

What are you *certain* of in your life? Are you *certain* that you love your children unconditionally? Are you *certain* that you are in a happy marriage? Are you *certain* that your body is healthy and perfect? Make a list of items you are *certain* of...and don't be surprised if this list is shorter than you expect!

As we analyze ourSelves in total truth, we see what things we think *may* be, but realize that we are not *certain* of them deep within our core. Then, put forth a certainty of something you desire. Begin with a short term experience: be *certain* that your boss will love your proposal; be *certain* that you will find that perfect dress in the first store you enter; be *certain* that you will pick the perfect day camp for your kids.

Are you *certain* that, within three years, you will move, or that you will have two children, or that you will create the job of your dreams? Go there with great expectation and the power within your heart. Create, as God, and with *certainty*. What you create with certainty will ultimately become your reality!

When we become certain regarding our health, then our body responds to that creation. This is a bit more challenging, for the mind throws doubt into this path of thought. You have the power to override your mind by acknowledging and releasing your doubt. If you are surrounded by nay-sayers, move them away from your life until you have completed your goal of healing. Are you *certain* that you will be healed? If so, then this will be your experience.

In your power, and with selfLove, ask that family and friends honor your choice to experience this true desire and challenge them to join you. Surround yourSelf with people who see you as healthy, even in the throes of adversity. Powerfully put forth your new choice to learn in ways that do not compromise your physical, mental, emotional or psychological aspects of Self. Feel your power as you know your certainty! Find your certainty within your heart! There are no mistakes, only lessons! Bring your body to its healing experience by knowing that you are perfect and powerful!

Exercises:

Releasing Fear

1. List your five greatest fears.

   a) For each fear, explain what your life would be like without it.

   b) For each fear, see yourSelf living without the fear and list three choices you would make if you didn't have that fear.

2. Choose to release these fears...and begin to make choices to live without them!

CHAPTER TEN

Self-Love vs. Self-Ish

Selfishness is rooted in fear.
SelfLove is rooted in acceptance!

It takes courage to move from illness-creation to total healing. In many lives, illness becomes an emotional tool of limitation, as well as control. One need not be as responsible in life (and living) if one is ill. People expect less of you. You do not need to work, perhaps, or commit to the fullness of a relationship.

When we are healthy, we have no excuse to do less; in fact, we think we must do more and more. We live in a society in which we feel obligated to stretch ourSelves into a myriad of arenas: we work, we raise our families, we maintain our homes, we volunteer, and we play hard. When you are ill, you receive more attention from parents, children or spouse. Once you become well, the responsibility for your life (and living) is your own! In many circumstances, this responsibility can be challenging. We leave ourSelves little time for relaxation and the care of Self. We put ourSelves at such low priority because, otherwise, our choices would be considered selfish.

SelfLove and selfishness are very different. As I work with people and tell them that they can experience selfLove, many times they worry that this will make them selfish. There is not so fine a line between the two. SelfLove is celebrating one's magnificence—in other words, always making choices based upon joy; energetically being in comfort with each thought, each desire

Identify a choice you wish to make simply to experience joy.

List the impact you perceive this choice will have on those in your life. Pick one or two of these individuals and discuss your perception of their reaction and how it inhibits you. See if you will discover that they would be happy for your choice to experience joy in this manner.

and each action; loving oneSelf enough to choose from love; honoring Self and *other as Self* in every moment of Being. In selfishness, there is no honor for Self or for others. Selfish choices are based in fear, anger or separation. One chooses to *limit* the experience of love within a selfish act—for Self and for the other. Selfishness is the hoarding of energy; selfLove is sharing energy, even though it may not be apparent in the moment of action.

SelfLove involves acceptance, truth, celebration and love. Selfishness involves anger, fear, separation and absence of shared energy. When making a choice in selfLove, you are honoring Self, regardless of the reactions of others. Actions created in selfLove leave you comfortable, because your choices honor your joy. Selfishness leaves uncomfortable feelings within all involved, even the person performing the action for him or herSelf. Selfishness removes the connection between people, whereas selfLove ultimately creates new, stronger relationships.

Meg* was having an extremely difficult time with her mother, a widow who demanded all of Meg's free time. Unmarried, Meg lived nearby and catered to her mother's every whim. Meg worked full time and would visit her mother after work each day. She would mow her mother's lawn, empty the trash cans, clean her mother's house and then go home and do the same for herSelf.

Interestingly, Meg had a sister and a brother who visited their mother less often and chose not to help in this fashion. Meg was overburdened by this responsibility, but when I suggested alternatives, such as hiring people to help, she balked, saying that her mother would refuse assistance from "strangers." Meg believed that she was being unselfish, and if selfLove meant that she would not be there to do everything her mother wished, then she would be a selfish daughter.

Meg complained bitterly that her sister and brother were too selfish to help. This was an interesting scenario. I explained to Meg that the selfishness here was on the part of her mother, that if her mother were experiencing selfLove, she would honor all of her children and allow them to live their lives fully. I also challenged Meg about her own selfLove. Was she performing these chores from a sense of love or duty? Was she doing them in joy or in anger? I told her I believed that her siblings were emotionally healthier than she, in that they were able to choose for themSelves the kind of lives they wanted to live. I challenged Meg to stop working for her mother and watch her sister and brother come forward to assist by making outside arrangements for the mowing and housework.

However, Meg was too entrenched in this creation. Meg's mother made a fuss if things were not going her way, and Meg was afraid of these outbursts. She was being manipulated and was angry that her sister and brother were free. This all came down to their personal choice.

Meg did not love herSelf enough to feel worthy of living a full and joyful life. Her siblings wanted more than being tied down to their selfish parent. They were honorable in other aspects, calling their mother frequently and celebrating family functions together. However, they were moving strongly towards their own freedom, something Meg has never experienced by her own choosing. Meg was deeply in need of her mother's approval and totally tied up in her mother's drama of helplessness. Would it have been selfish of Meg to change her life? Would her mother not have adjusted to having assistance from others? When would this dance come to an end?

The reason Meg came to me in the first place was due to her physical ailments. These ailments were all rooted in the emotional and psychological limitations Meg had allowed herSelf to become entwined in. She was also creating illness to get out of doing so much work, hoping deep down that her sister and brother would step forward to help out of a sense of duty.

Sadly, Meg was going from healer to healer to heal her body, but was unwilling to work through the issues which were at the heart of her physical creation of illness. She would end our session empowered and stronger, then immediately go to her mother's home to complete her chores, thus moving instantly to accepting her powerlessness once again. Meg did not take action to make the necessary changes in her life that would allow her to experience her own freedom. She could not understand that selfLove would free both herSelf and her mother, and so the game continued.

Selfishness is rooted in fear. SelfLove is an act of acceptance. Acts of selfLove manifest joy. Freedom exists for all of us but is most powerfully manifested from the loving of Self. True and total healing of body, mind and spirit occurs once a person chooses to experience selfLove fully. In loving ourSelves, we then manifest experiences which reflect this love.

During our sessions, many people tell me that they love themSelves. Barbara* believed she loved herSelf, because she honored her body by eating well, exercising and working only part time. She was in a comfortable marriage and had no financial problems. Life was fun for Barbara, and yet, she had manifested chronic fatigue syndrome. She struggled with this ailment for many years, as do many women in our society.

Barbara had many friends and a large family, and prided herSelf on always being available when someone needed her. She was the first to volunteer her services, unaware that she was being overwhelmed by responsibilities which she took upon herSelf on behalf of others. In working together, we broke down Barbara's day-to-day activities, and she suddenly realized how little time she ever reserved for herSelf.

I presented her with the challenge of choosing only out of selfLove, and when she understood the core element of loving herSelf and choosing total joy, Barbara recognized that many of her obligations were simply...obligations!

They were joyless actions on her part, done simply out of her personal sense of duty.

Part of Barbara's healing was to disengage from all people for a number of weeks. This was quite challenging, for she was truly a people-person and loved them all. However, in total selfLove, she followed the requirement of cutting off all outside communication and allowed herSelf to rediscover her personal joys. Suddenly, she had time to do things she wanted to do, rather than things she thought she *had* to do!

Barbara's healing was profound in many ways. Not only were her friends and family supportive, but she saw that they were able to survive without her. Although this was disconcerting at first, Barbara quickly learned that doing for others could be by her choice, without obligation, and that everyone would survive if she were to refuse to take on responsibility that was too much for her.

Barbara was able to recognize that she was not being selfish when she refused to help out another person the moment they asked. Rather, she learned that, by honoring herSelf, she was also honoring the other, for doing a favor with resentment honors neither, while declining in a loving, honoring manner honors both. Barbara's physical healing was a powerful consequence of her new choices, because, once she experienced selfLove, her body resonated in this new vibration, and her self-creation profoundly changed.

We have been taught since childhood that to love ourSelves is selfish. This belief should be released, so we can experience the joy that we are. It takes courage to make choices in selfLove. When we are whole and recognize the perfection of ourSelves, we then live our lives in our truth. Loving oneSelf simply allows for greater love to enter each relationship we have.

...and we begin to heal, through love.

Exercises:

Choosing Through SelfLove

1. List the activities you choose for yourSelf which bring you joy. How often do you experience these activities?

2. Are there obligations in your life that you resent? Are you willing to let them go?

3. Are you willing to commit to a two-hour block of time each week just for you?
   a) What would you do with this time?
   b) Does the thought of it fill you with peace and joy?
   c) Will you make the time to do it? Begin NOW!

CHAPTER ELEVEN

Acknowledging Your Truth

Our truth is how we live, not what we dream of or believe we are.

While growing up, most of us were told the importance of always telling the truth...and we were usually punished for our lies. Ironically, as children, we often witnessed the "Do as I say, not as I do" rule, which was a bit confusing to the young mind. At least, this was my personal experience.

As I mentioned earlier in the book, it was important for me to speak my truth, especially when working with clients and guiding them spiritually. There were occasional times when the client did not want to hear the truth, and so I kept silent. I always honored their freedom of choice without judgment and without further thought.

As I experienced my creation of illness, I knew that, throughout its development, I had been lying to mySelf. I was also in powerful judgment of mySelf, believing that I was living a dual life by creating illness in my own body while still assisting clients with their creations of pain. In addition, I did not want to face the possibility of having a disease as frightening as cancer growing in my body. And, as I lied to mySelf, I lied to everyone around me. They thought something was wrong, but they, too, really did not want to face such a powerful experience of pain. And so, we all kept silent.

There are many moments in our lives when we choose not to face personal truths. This is because we judge our choices so harshly that we experience them as pain and do not want to face that pain for a moment

Look at your life and identify how you live a dual life – one public and one private. In what ways do you behave differently?

Look at the underlying issues in your heart that lead you to make such choices. Now be aware of your choice to act differently and make a new choice so that you can change this pattern of self-diminishment.

longer than we have to. Unfortunately, this choice almost cost me my life. Until my body could no longer function normally, I chose to remain in a self-created bubble of lies regarding my state of health. I was, for a very long time, hiding from mySelf.

Most people think they are truthful. They are honest, and confuse honesty with truth. We are upstanding citizens, who work hard, pay taxes and go shopping with hard-earned dollars. For the most part, we do not cheat or steal. And those who do and get caught are scorned by society.

Living in truth is acknowledging who you are and not hiding any part of Self from yourSelf. I always thought I was living this way, until my illness began to rear its head. Then I did not want to know and believed I was disguising my personal truth from everyone, including me.

On a deeper level, we may think we know who and what we are, but most of us actually live in a state of denial. It challenges us to examine all of our choices and face our reality. We don't want to be responsible for our actions...or our reactions. We want to eat what we want, drink what we want, say and do what we want and not be responsible for the effects of these choices on our bodies, our hearts or our lives.

Clayton* is a kind and generous man, gifted in the holistic healing arts and very giving of his time and energy. He presents the appearance of living fully self-empowered, for, in his work, he teaches empowerment to others. He assists clients with challenging issues in their lives, guiding them peacefully and teaching them selfLove.

However, his private life is filled with self-doubt, and he allows himSelf outbursts of anger and frustration which he holds in check with non-family members. Clayton claims to be quite joyous, but is in denial regarding the differences in his behavior with his family versus his clients. He insists that he experiences selfLove, even when I show him that he does not by offering examples of his personal life-choices which were based on lack and fear.

Clayton refuses to acknowledge his truth, and by refusing to accept it, he cannot release his core issue and allow himSelf to live fully. He is happy in this moment of his existence, and I can only remind him of the greater joys he would experience once he looks into the mirror and accepts his truth.

Many times, I work with clients who do not want to admit who they are, because they are in powerful judgment of themSelves. I've worked with women who would not face the pain they experienced because of sexual affairs they chose while still married...or even the pain that led them to this choice. Other clients will not acknowledge the pain that leads them to choose alcohol, or marijuana use. And some will not admit to the pain they are experiencing within their marriages, fearful that it would require major changes in their lives. It is not that they must immediately change the circumstances of their lives; the healing begins by simply acknowledging the truth.

Some people live in their own little world of "make-believe," not realizing that such choice creates limitation, thereby preventing them from fully loving themSelves. It is not only that which we judge to be negative that we will not admit to. In many instances, we find it hard to admit that we are all-powerful and responsible for everything *wonderful* that occurs in our lives, because we believe that to do so is egotistical! Once we understand that accepting responsibility for *all* that we create is simply acknowledging our power, and that all people are equally powerful, then we can face the truth of our creations and change those we no longer wish to experience.

To live a life of truth—and in celebration of that truth—is to live fully in selfLove. To recognize that there are areas of our lives in which we feel less comfortable than others is simply a recognition of Self. Some of us are stronger with numbers than others. Some of us write and communicate better. Some are more scientifically driven, while others enjoy the arts. This does not mean that we should diminish those aspects of Being which we do not excel at or do not enjoy. To acknowledge all that we are is honorable and loving. We can accept all that we are and choose to continue living as we have been, or we can choose to change our patterns. Both choices are equally admirable and acceptable, as long as the choice is made through self-acceptance and selfLove.

Truthfulness goes hand in hand with mindfulness. We need to choose to look at ourSelves fully and without judgment in all moments of our lives. We do not need to publicize who we are, and privacy is always a choice. However, we can know ourSelves fully and accept all of our choices and our personalities without judging them as not being perfect...for everything *is* perfect, just as it is. As we look into our hearts and choose an aspect of Self we no longer want to experience, we can then choose to change it. If we never look, then we do not give ourSelves the opportunity for change.

One of the most challenging things to admit about ourSelves is that we are in judgment. Most of us are, and we have lived this way for so long that we no longer recognize this part of ourSelves. We are often in powerful judgment of Self. How often have you heard yourSelf say, "I can't believe how clumsy I am," or "I'm getting fat as a cow." "I can't figure that out because I'm not smart enough," or "You can't teach an old dog new tricks." Of course, there are also the expressions we use when we talk about others, such as, "Who does she think she is, wearing that?" or "He didn't deserve that promotion." The list is endless, and we have all, at one time or another, chosen such expressions about Self or others in a diminishing fashion.

When we choose to live in truth, we listen more carefully to our words and are more aware of our thoughts. *Our truth is how we live, not what we dream of or believe we are.* We are God as pain, just as much as we are God as joy. Not acknowledging what we *are* diminishes us.

As I experienced the healing of my body, I chose to heal my heart, as well, in order to *fully* heal. This was the path to total healing, and this is what I wanted. I chose to look at mySelf with a magnifying glass, asking those closest to me to assist me with this choice. It took courage on their parts to help me face painful aspects of mySelf, but their love was so powerful and the desire to share my healing so great that the experience was always one of love and honor.

I will use mySelf as an example of what it means to know truth of Self, for in this discovery, we must look at all that we are most anxious to hide from the world. Throughout my life, until the healing of my heart, I had difficulty accepting compliments. For example, whenever someone told me that I was beautiful or smart, I became uncomfortable. I would not acknowledge my beauty, always finding a flaw in mySelf. I would not admit that I was intelligent, even though I knew I was. I never felt lovable, always believing that those who loved me were obligated to do so, mostly because we were related. I didn't trust friendships, because I couldn't understand why anyone who was *not* related to me could love me!

I was also very much in judgment of the medical community, believing that alternative methods were better. I had promised mySelf I would never undergo chemotherapy, not knowing that one day that choice would be placed before me, and that I would have to powerfully go into my heart and choose to release my fears and beliefs, in order to fully heal my body.

During this time of healing, I was also challenged to look at how privately I lived my life. I always wanted to hide, never wanting to be in the spotlight. And yet, I was driven to write this book, knowing that one day it would place me in the public eye. What a fascinating creation of contradicting desires!

I had to deeply explore my heart and make the choice of accepting the public airing of my life, having previously shared little of my life with the outside world. It was an important and powerful moment for me to explore my truth. I had to deal with my fears about what the world would think of my choosing to share my personal story, including the airing of my family secrets. Would I enjoy the spotlight? Would I judge mySelf if I did? Was it acceptable to me, in my heart, to publicly share my whole story?

Having a colostomy is a private and personal experience, and when the body is altered in such a huge fashion, we tend to want to hide from the world. That's how it was for me in the beginning. But, as I recognized the power of my story—the creation and the healing of my illness—I knew that standing tall with a colostomy and living a life of selfLove would honor me and others. It took months for me to make the choice that I made. This choice was not made lightly. But I made it in my love for mySelf.

So how do I see mySelf, now that I am living in truth? I see my beauty, and I honor my intelligence. I accept and celebrate the love of friends and family. I am as wonderful a friend to others as they are towards me and comfortably accept the love we share. I honor all choices and accept all pathways of life and living. I listen to my words carefully, so that I catch mySelf when expressing judgment. Most importantly, I love mySelf fully, and I know who I am. I am God. Powerful. Perfect. Magnificent. Beautiful. Just like you.

It is important to recognize that I, personally, made this choice to live in truth. Not everyone chooses to do so...and they are aware of their unwillingness. This does not make them dishonest; it simply acknowledges their fear of being "found out." That they do not acknowledge the perfection of who they are is a reflection of their belief that they are not perfect. They are in self-judgment, and in "hiding." This choice is honored. However, when we choose to live in limitation, we choose to experience less than the greatest joys selfLove can offer.

When I ask people their truth, they sometimes do not even recognize that they cannot see it. We must choose to not judge ourSelves or feel shame because of choices we have made. All moments are opportunities to learn and accept or change that which we are. There are no mistakes, no "right" and no "wrong." There simply is what is—and when we look at ourSelves with eyes of acceptance and neutrality, we can willingly live fully in truth in all moments, allowing our bodies and our spirits to be free of the blocks that create the disharmonies of our lives.

Exercises:
Acknowledging Your Truth

1. List five things about yourSelf you are least willing to share with others.
   a) Acknowledge, honor, and celebrate them.
   b) Release your judgment of them.
   c) Release the choice to keep them a secret.

2. Recognize how you have learned from these choices you have made, and choose how you will live from this moment forth.

CHAPTER TWELVE

Are You Listening?

We have all the answers we ever need within our hearts.
That is called our "knowing."

We live in a world filled with noise—noise coming from our children, our television sets, our stereos, construction on the roads, planes flying overhead...and even from our own thoughts. Most of us relish the moments of silence in our lives—after the lights are out at night before sleep, or in the early morning before the household wakes up, or as we sit on a rock during a hike in the mountains or at the seashore. Sometimes we crave silence in our busy world, but all too often we forget to make the time to just sit...and be.

There are always answers to all questions of our hearts. Answers come in all ways, but to hear them we must choose to learn how to listen. If you have a question in your heart, the answer may come to you an hour, a day or a month later. Sometimes it is through the words of a stranger. Sometimes it is a song on the radio. Sometimes even the innocent conversation of a child. If you learn how to listen to the world around you, you will discover all that you ever need to know. And when you learn to listen to your inner voice, you will discern truth from desire, fear and judgment.

In order to hear your inner voice, choose to silence your thoughts, so that your heart can speak. Our hearts speak to us always, but many of us are too busy, too distracted by our daily lives, to listen. Know that this is a choice, for it takes but a moment to silence our thoughts and hear the knowing that comes from within.

We have all the answers we ever need within our hearts. That is called our "knowing." Sometimes we have difficulty accessing our inner knowing, because we influence the outcome with our desire. When we remain in a neutral state of Being, then we can more easily discern what we are trying to communicate to ourSelves.

You will not hear your inner voice if you choose to talk a lot. Regardless of the words shared, whether they are loving or not, constant talking interferes with your ability to listen to yourSelf and others. Recognize also that, whether you are speaking out loud or to yourSelf in silence, you cannot, while speaking, be listening! You can only accomplish one of these tasks at a time, so in order to listen, silence must exist within and without your Being.

Elizabeth* was a most loving person, always wanting to reach out and help a person in need. She was greatly loved for her generous nature, but she was unable to recognize that her greatest limitation was her inability to maintain silence for more than a moment at a time. This situation prevented Elizabeth from hearing what other people wanted to share with her. Gradually, those close to her went more and more into their own silence in her presence, and they also began to tune her out.

This had great impact on Elizabeth's family. One of her children withdrew into himSelf and rarely offered information to her unless she pried it out of him. Another child became a screamer, needing desperately to be heard but often "talked over" by his mother. Disagreements with her husband were challenging, because Elizabeth talked faster and faster when angered or frustrated, leaving the communication between them blocked. Sometimes family members were unable to finish their sentences before Elizabeth would cut in, offering her advice and suggestions. She did this in an effort to help them, not recognizing that, instead, she was hindering their efforts to communicate with her. Even in social situations, Elizabeth would interrupt another person and go off on a tangent, not realizing that she was listening to herSelf in her head and ignoring the subject being shared by others.

What was fascinating to me was that, when working with Elizabeth on other issues in her life, I found it challenging to complete my thoughts, since she would interrupt me mid-sentence. She was fully unaware of this behavior, and when it was pointed out to her, she would be surprised and quiet...for a while. Unfortunately, her patterned behavior was quite powerful, so she needed to choose to make a conscious effort to be in silence, learning to listen while others spoke to her and responding with a softer and more concise choice of words.

It is important to acknowledge our patterns, without judgment and without self-criticism. Constant talking can represent a need to control, or an underlying fear. A fear of being ignored, or invisible. A fear of being unimportant. Or a fear of suddenly discovering, through the words of others, who we truly are.

When working with Madeline*, I recognized that her issue involved speaking words about herSelf which were untrue. Madeline always wanted to "fit in," so she would use words she thought would make those around her more comfortable. She did not perceive that, by doing so, she was, in effect, lying. In many instances, her friends were insulted by her diminishment of herSelf, and of them, by this manner of speaking.

Madeline was not aware of this pattern of behavior. For example, she was financially quite comfortable and enjoyed shopping for a new wardrobe at each change of season. However, even though she purchased designer

Watch your word choices. Listen to yourSelf, and others, speak.

Do you speak in a positive and pro-active manner, or do your words reflect doom and gloom? Do you talk a lot, or do you tend to hold back thoughts from others? Do you make time to listen to your knowing, or do you fill your space with music and other noise?

Pay attention to your choices and discover the joy of the silence of your heart.

clothing for herSelf and her family, she denied knowing anything about famous designers, feigning an inability to afford such luxuries. Her friends, well aware of Madeline's wardrobe, did not know what to make of such statements.

In other instances, she would complain about her financial issues, often to those around her who were experiencing financial challenges of their own. Madeline probably meant well, perhaps wanting to make these others feel more comfortable. However, she was unaware that the others were well aware of her truth, and they were uncomfortable with her words of lack and, ultimately, with Madeline.

A side effect of Madeline's lack of self-awareness regarding her pattern of speaking involved the way she discussed others. Madeline would never label herSelf a "gossip," but because she spoke so thoughtlessly, she would criticize her friends and others close to her without ever realizing it. She also thoughtlessly shared personal stories which others had shared with her in confidence, without ever recognizing that she was doing so.

Wally* was an interesting client, for he would ask a question, and as soon as I began to respond, he would ask another. And another. I was literally unable to complete a sentence. I chose to attempt to remain silent until he noticed, but then, when I resumed talking, he would interrupt again. It took quite an effort to point this out to him. He laughed, but made the choice to learn how to listen. Wally's whole life began to change when he acknowledged his patterns and chose to change them.

Understand, however, that it takes more than silence to allow us to learn to listen. People who rarely speak are not necessarily good listeners. People who are quiet sometimes get lost in their thoughts, or do not care to share the conversation which is occurring around them and sometimes simply "wander off." A quiet person may be one who is dealing with insecurities about themSelves in a crowd, or who feels inadequate with the subject at hand. A quiet person may also be expressing their desire to separate themSelves from others, choosing their own company rather than that of others. These people choose not to listen; instead, they live in their own personal creations in their heads, disconnecting from the world around them.

It is important to choose to stop and listen to yourSelf, as well as to others. We do not need to say things to make others feel better; many times people share issues with us simply to have a voice. Silence is a great gift we can share with another. In a loving and sensitive fashion, we each can choose to allow our friends and family members the opportunity to express their emotions without our need to jump in and "make it all better." We cannot "make it all better." We can simply make it easier for them by giving them a sounding board when they seek it.

We should also acknowledge that the words of another offer an opportunity for us to learn about ourSelves. We are all One. Because of this truth, there are no words shared that do not have an impact upon Self. When in conversation, always make the time to reflect upon the words offered by others. Understand that, in each moment, you are being given information that reflects back to you a manifestation of how you are choosing to love yourSelf. When others speak, it is "you" talking to "you." What are you trying to tell yourSelf?

We can choose to always speak words of truth, but to do so, we must know who we are. Some people change personalities, depending upon whom they are speaking to in the moment. Some people are kinder to strangers than to their loved ones. Others choose to enjoy conversations with friends but are silent within their families, or vice versa. We can recognize that, in all moments, what we say and how we listen honors Self and other in that moment of experience.

Listening well is an art which can be learned easily. It is a choice we can make to bring greater peace to our lives. We can listen with interest in experiencing other people, celebrating them and letting go of all judgment, so they can speak in safety. We use words in all moments, and through our words, we create our realities.

Watch your word choices. Listen to yourSelf, and others, speak. Do you speak in a positive and pro-active manner, or do your words reflect doom and gloom? Do you talk a lot, or do you tend to hold back thoughts from others? Do you make time to listen to your knowing, or do you fill your space with music and other noise? Pay attention to your choices and discover the joy of the silence of your heart.

Exercise:
Learning to Listen

1. If you have a tendency to talk a lot, make a powerful choice to discover your silence.
   a) Put aside some time—a day, a week or a month—and choose to speak only when necessary.
   b) Do not phone anyone. Simply respond to the calls you receive, and speak minimally, focusing instead on listening.
   c) Listen to your word choices and the subjects being shared.
   d) Take great care and speak without exaggeration or about another person.
   e) Focus on the person with whom you are speaking, and discover what they truly want through the conversation at hand.
   f) Do not offer advice. Offer, instead, your comforting presence.

The longer you choose to do this exercise, the more you will see changes in yourSelf and those closest to you.

2. If you have a tendency to be silent, make a powerful choice to share your stories.

    a) Over the next few days, week or month, tell different people different things about yourSelf.

    b) Feel free to discuss incidents from your childhood, or dreams regarding your future.

    c) Talk about yourSelf only, making a point of sharing something your listener did not know about you.

The longer you choose to do this exercise, the more comfortable you will become in interacting with others.

3. Focus on the way you speak to others, and understand that, in all conversation, you are talking to yourSelf.

    a) How do you speak to yourSelf?

    b) What are you trying to tell yourSelf?

    c) What types of words do you use?

    d) What are you learning?

    e) What does the conversation say about how you love yourSelf?

CHAPTER THIRTEEN

Healer Dependency, Healer Abuse

*You are your greatest healer. No one can heal you but **you!***

We live in a society filled with healing opportunities which have never existed before. Diseases are annihilated, and created, all the time. Lots of money is dedicated to research to cure and control illness, and the technologies of our time allow for great strides in the battle against powerful diseases. In addition, ancient healing arts are being reawakened and used throughout the planet, increasing the rate of successful healing for those struggling with health challenges.

Given all that is now available, people experiencing illness can recognize that, in most cases, the cure for their disease exists. When medical technology is combined with their power to make choices that will heal their hearts, they can allow their bodies to heal. Many choose to forego medical technologies and believe they can holistically heal themSelves.

We are all-powerful, but all that exists is a manifestation of our power, not a crutch or sign of weakness. Honoring all healing pathways as equal allows for healing. We should not choose to ignore modern technology, for it, too, aids the physical body in healing. By combining modern medicine and inner release, the root of the illness can be determined, and the person can then be healed more quickly and profoundly.

By the time she was guided to work with me, Felicia* was close to losing her battle with cancer. She had a large tumor on her neck, which was threatening to close off her jugular vein. Felicia was terrified of chemotherapy, having had severe side effects in a breast-cancer battle ten years earlier. There were two important issues here. First, why did Felicia manifest a second bout of cancer in her body? Second, chemotherapy was a necessary treatment, which she needed to undergo in order to survive, and she had to overcome her fear in order to save her own life!

Felicia spent a lot of money seeking alternative therapies all over the country, none of which was fully capable of removing the cancer itself. As the illness took on stronger proportions, she was becoming totally disabled and powerfully more stubborn. I explained to her that all things are of God, even chemotherapy. It is essential to make use of all options available to us without prejudice. Ultimately, Felicia did indeed go to an oncologist, and three months later, her tumor had shrunk down to a manageable size. From here, we began to work on the energies at play and her prognosis became one of complete healing.

Healing involves a three-way marriage between medical healer, alternative healer and patient. This is *complementary healing*. Western medicine offers us the opportunity to remove a symptom of illness in a short period of time. Of course, when medications are prescribed as a matter of course, the patient can choose to powerfully search within his or her own body and soul to determine if that form of treatment will create the healing they seek. If a simple prescription can bring relief or even a cure, this would be a step along the path to total healing.

Check each of the following healing modalities that you would be willing to experience in order to heal:

surgery____

pharmaceuticals____

acupuncture____

chiropractics____

energy healing____

herbal supplements____

Chinese medicine____

aromatherapy____

medical treatment____

psychotherapy____

rolfing____

massage____

nutritional changes____

other alternatives____

Which ones are you hesitant about? Why? Choose to release your judgment and accept all methods of healing as equal.

However, if one medication follows another in the hunt for a cure, a person can choose to use his or her free will and refuse that form of treatment. We are not pincushions unless we give permission to be! We should look upon doctors as people equal to ourSelves, educated in a field of their choosing that should bring them joy. If you go to a doctor who is devoid of happiness in his or her manner, think twice about allowing him or her to discern your wholeness of Being, for he/she has not found it in him/herSelf!

Another step in the process of healing is finding an alternative or *complementary* healer who can work with your ailment. Sometimes, this is even more complicated than finding a suitable physician, for there are a myriad of choices available. Recommendations by other people struggling with ailments parallel to your own are a perfect way to uncover a new path towards healing. However, you should feel within your heart that this path will allow for profound change within your life, because, ultimately, you will be responsible for your own healing experience. A holistic healer is one who simply jump-starts your body onto a new pathway, reminding the energy flow of the body to reclaim its power. The body then has the opportunity to heal more than only the physical, since the energy affects all aspects of one's Being, including the mind and the spirit. Your thoughts and feelings about the holistic method are powerful enhancements—or deterrents—to your healing, and you can choose to approach this process from a state of total acceptance and allowance.

Understand that, whatever healing approach you choose, you will gain great learning in the process. Nothing occurs without purpose, and the learning offers you the opportunity to make new choices.

In working with both the medical physician and/or the holistic practitioner, the most powerful impetus to total healing is YOU! You should always be pro-active when allowing the knowledge of another to create a new paradigm in your life. Regardless of how minor or serious the illness, you are ultimately your own healer! If you suffer from allergies, for example, they will always return from season to season, if you believe that this will be so. Medicine will relieve the symptoms, but what of the emotional creation behind these allergies?

Always seek out a healing practitioner who knows that the cause of illness comes from *within*. There are methods available which blame circumstances on energies or experiences *outside* of you, but you should understand that what is *outside* is never the root of the issue.

I know a fellow alternative practitioner, Joe*, with whom I've struggled with this basic concept. He always works with what he calls "entities," which, he claims, attack a person and whose release allows the person to heal. This is a fear-based belief system, and, from this belief, he creates a situation in which he finds these "entities" when working with a client.

Joe never could understand why he was unable to quit his job and go into his healing practice full time. In fact, Joe is so entrenched in this belief system, and so powerfully refuses to acknowledge his own participation in this creation, that he manifested illness within his body, which he blames on an "attack" from another person. When I offered him my services, he turned me down, because he was unable to accept that he created this energy in his own body. His rage was palpable towards this "enemy," and I chose to give him the space to learn great truth in his own time and experience.

Healing practitioners, whether medical or holistic, should experience total joy with their work. Consider their appearance and their energies of healthfulness and peacefulness, for they share themSelves in the work they do with you. There should be a confidence in their own abilities and a powerful aspect of love in their words and energies, bringing you comfort and ease.

Just as you would think twice about going to a doctor who is obese and who abuses his body, you can choose to recognize the importance for all practitioners to *walk the talk*. If your marriage is falling apart, why go to a therapist who is in the process of getting a divorce? If your child requires emotional assistance, why consult a childless psychiatrist? Why go to a priest with your sexual issues? It is in making these choices that you can use your inner knowing and your true power...and choose, based upon the instinct we are each gifted with.

Holistic practitioners generally do not speak with fear-based terminology, as some medical doctors still do. You will never hear about the odds of failure; rather, you will only discuss the success of your healing. You may be challenged to make life changes during the healing program, but they are always for your greatest benefit and are shared without judgment. When seeking a complementary healer, pay attention to his or her words. If you are approached with a vocabulary that fills you with dread, then this healer is not tuned in to your true essence and will not serve you in your healing path.

It is imperative that we honor each other always. A holistic practitioner is generally more tuned in to your heart energy than is a medical doctor, simply because that is a major aspect of the holistic program. A healer should not offer you a pat explanation in describing his or her work; rather, they should always speak directly, addressing your energy, your needs, your fears and your strengths. This is intuitive, and if the healer does not acknowledge you as a whole and powerful individual, then they are simply going through the motions and are not relying on their own inner guidance in their work.

If you cannot reach the healing practitioner directly and must communicate through an office person, that person's energy is equally important, since it is the reflection of the healer him/herSelf. In other words, we should feel the energy of all involved, from the receptionist to the assistant, because their energies will reflect the energy of the person you are seeking.

I have been challenged by more than a few regarding receiving payment for "God's" work. *All work is God's work.* Whether you are a street sweeper or a lawyer, a token collector or a doctor, *you are God!* There is enough abundance for all, and if some choose to use natural gifts to assist the healing of those who are ill, that is simply a chosen method of employment.

More importantly, where is the exchange of energy when a healer works with a client and there is no payment? What value is perceived by the recipient of this energy work, if they do not have to contribute energetically?

When I charge for my time, the person makes a commitment to participate in the changes that will occur within them. And if one financially invests in their own healing, odds are greater that they will invest emotionally and actively!

And most importantly, the message here is that we *all* possess the ability to heal ourSelves, to hear messages from within and without, to see Truth in all things, to engage in love on every level! If some of us choose to share these abilities to help bring others to this same understanding, is this not invaluable?

Interestingly, our society has created a new brand of clients—spiritual hypochondriacs. There are a great many people who go from healer to healer, sometimes also from doctor to doctor, seeking relief from physical, energetic, spiritual or mental symptoms, unwilling to partner in the healing process by accepting responsibility for their own lives and choices.

Some are so engrossed in this drama that they never follow through with one set of directions before beginning another, interfering in all ways with the healing. One client I had, Marsha*, called me for a session to work on an intestinal disorder she had been struggling with for a number of months. Unbeknownst to me, she was already under the care of a nutritionist, who had her on a parasite program. Prior to working with him, Marsha had worked with another energy healer, whose process needed two months to complete. Each of us independently told her that she needed to follow a specific regimen for a number of weeks, yet she never allowed the prescribed time period to be completed before she began seeking another source of healing.

Marsha was in total fear of her symptoms and kept looking for someone who could do the work for her that she was unwilling to do for herSelf. She also kept blaming the healers for their failures, not coming to terms with her own responsibility for sabotaging her own healing path.

Many people seek holistic methods of healing as a "magic pill," just as they go to medical professionals for the medicine that will make them well. There is no such thing. Medicines work best when dealing with a temporary viral or bacterial condition, but when working through a major ailment, there are always emotional and energetic roots which should be cleared out, in order to allow the body a profound healing opportunity. If a person develops pneumonia, they can be physically healed, but this will always leave their lungs in a weakened state. However, once the root of the creation of the illness—in this case a feeling of being smothered—is released consciously and energetically, then the lung system of the body has the opportunity to be strengthened and will no longer be the source of discomfort.

In order to uncover the root, many emotions come into play. Perhaps the client is dealing with a difficult marriage, or an overbearing parent, or too many responsibilities between home and work, etc. Any or all of these aspects of life can create the feeling of being smothered or the inability to breathe. The magic pill here is simply the person's choice! What are they going to change in their life in order to free themSelves and live more fully? Medical practices will heal the symptoms, as will many holistic methods, but it is important to recognize that new choices need to be made, in order to bring that person's life to greater peace and a healthier experience of living.

Over time, because our bodies will ultimately reflect the pain we hold deep in our hearts, illness is created. When we love ourSelves, we honor all pathways to healing, acknowledging the importance of bringing mind, body and spirit into balance. The medical model focuses on the physical body; the holistic choices assist us in clearing the energies and emotions rooted in pain; and the choice to live differently in order to honor Self in love enables the healing to be profound. Be empowered when working with another person, whether they are a medical doctor or a complementary healing practitioner.

You are your greatest healer. No one can heal you but *you!* Participate fully, make new choices, love and honor yourSelf, and live a life filled with joy, peace and health.

Exercises:
Choices for Wellness

1. Write a brief description of the last time you were sick.
   a) What did you do?
   b) Where did you seek assistance?
   c) What did you change in your life to promote your healing?

2. Have you made any new choices in your life which you have maintained in order to continue to experience wellness?

CHAPTER FOURTEEN

Experience Total Healing
Body, Mind and Spirit

Love is not an exchange between two people.
It is the embracing in joy and awe of oneSelf as perfect.
It is the letting go of everything but the love of Self.
Nothing else sustains the physical.

In my healing practice, I work with a magnificent partner—my dear friend Christine Lenick. Chris is especially gifted in her work with the soul. Chris has the ability to receive direct communication from each person's soul, plus detailed instructions on healing the physical. She also teaches people how to live in this moment in joy, regardless of present-life circumstances, by making choices based in selfLove.

In conversation one day, we were looking for a definition of healing. Chris shared the following communication through meditation:

Healing is a letting go. In the instant we fully know we are God, we let go of all limitation, and healing is not just of the physical. It is of the body, mind and spirit. When we hold on to anything except our total love of Self, we limit the energetic flow of pure love. When we limit anything, we create a block to creation. Creation is without form or constraint. It is the energy of pure knowing and it just is.

Healing of the mind and spirit occurs with release of all constraint. Neither the mind nor the spirit has any bounds, except that, when perceived to be so, they are in that moment created. So, to heal, we must let go of everything by which we define ourSelves and our lives. Imagine yourSelf like a balloon that can expand forever and float forever. Watch yourSelf do so, and observe the first point at which you think that balloon will break or hit something and pop. That is how you create limits now with yourSelf. The balloon will never pop unless you see it doing so.

So many on the Earth plane focus on healing of the physical. The physical is just the picture we paint with our choices. When we choose through any choice made in judgment of Self as less than all that we are, we create energetic damming and thereby physical change. We focus so much energy on this physical change, only drawing more damming energy to it. We should choose to focus instead on removing the dams. Let go of your fears, hate, disdain, judgment, abuse, unworthiness, etc. Challenge your soul to manifest by making life choices out of selfLove and nothing more. Such a soul will fight back, and you will need to release that energy. Acknowledge, release, accept, know with certainty. Embark on living your life and all will be presented to you.

I received a call from a woman who was seeking healing of a few minor ailments. We set an appointment, and she began the session by announcing that she wanted nothing more than the release of her physical symptoms. She proceeded to tell me that she was a great Being ("Aren't we all?" I challenged her), and that most other people were "vermin." She then asked me to teach her how to protect herSelf from the "vermin" all around her and that I also work with her on her loneliness issues.

She was quite serious and I approached her with courtesy and respect, gently challenging her choice of words and view of the world around her.

Very quickly and strongly, she advised me that I shouldn't waste my time trying to change her mind or her views of life, but that I should stick with the work at hand.

I refused to continue the session, explaining that we are all healed in combination of body, mind and spirit, and one cannot heal without all aspects of their Being being brought to issue. Not only was she seeking a magic pill, but she was unwilling to change core beliefs and personal paradigms which were at the root of the circumstances of her life.

As human beings, we are an amalgam of different experiences of Self. Much has been written on the triad of body, mind and spirit, and an important truth is that there is no separation. You are what you think and your body reflects that creation. A perfect flow, reflecting the wholeness of Being.

In the interpretation of signals put forth by our physical body, we analyze ourSelves in two ways: by thinking and by feeling. We know when we do not feel well, and, in many instances, the body shows physical symptoms, even abstractly, such as signs of weakness or tiredness. We then begin to *think* about what is wrong with us and use our minds to review any aspect of life we have experienced or read about as a basis to form a conclusion regarding the physical disharmony. Other times, we simply allow our *feelings* to warn us if it is serious or not, and we base our choices upon the combination of all three.

When choosing to heal through love, one automatically recognizes the spiritual component of healing the physical. How does one define love, since it is experienced as an emotion, not of the mind—and, in truth, it confuses thought—and not of the body, although the body directly responds to the stimuli that love creates.

Love is not an exchange between two people. It is the embracing in joy and awe of oneSelf as perfect. It is letting go of everything but love of Self. Nothing else sustains the physical.

— Our Bodies —

We put much emphasis upon the physical aspects of our lives—the homes we live in, the cars we choose to drive, the clothing we wear...and the bodies we have created. This is not to say that we must ignore these things; rather, we can choose to recognize that they are a reflection of our choices, and whenever we do not honor ourSelves, the physical will, at some point, begin to break down. However, the physical body has a purpose that we have ignored for too long; the physical body is the vehicle which houses our experience of Self.

Imagine your body to be a suit of clothing that reflects the choices of how you experience yourSelf. If you are not careful, you can tear the fabric of this piece of clothing, and then it must be mended in order to be able to be worn again. You should take great care to prevent your body from being damaged, and when damage occurs, you can choose to fix it, so that it can continue to move forward, housing the magnificence of your inner Being. If you do not meet its needs through food, water and exercise, it begins to weaken or break down. If you leave it unmended, then the damage may increase with time, perhaps becoming irreparable.

The human body is a fascinating piece of machinery. Thousands of cells make up the whole, each cell having a function that creates the energy that allows the individual system to function perfectly. The cells of your lungs are nothing like the cells of your heart; the cells of the skin are nothing like the cells of your blood. Each cellular system works within its own space of Being. They function together within the unity of each organ system, yet separately from other aspects of the physical. However, all the cells of the body work with a common goal—to give life to the wholeness of the physical body they are a part of.

The physical body has a total consciousness, and we often do not honor that consciousness. Each cell is an aspect of the whole, and it is important to look at the whole when dealing with imbalance in one aspect of the body. For instance, if a person has a tumor, the whole body has a tumor, not simply that particular body part. By viewing the body as a whole, you will choose a more holistic (or "wholistic") approach to your healing, thus honoring your body on all levels.

How many people talk to their bodies? How often do you tell it how wondrous it is...how beautiful...how perfect!? More importantly, how many people *listen* to their bodies? Do you not listen to your body when you feel thirsty? Thirst is simply a communication from body to mind that action is required to feed the cells much-needed liquid. Why is it inconceivable that, all things being God, there is great consciousness within all aspects of Being?

You should always choose to honor the physical Self. You have the ability to have a dialogue with your body, and your body will always respond. The body serves great purpose in the experience of Self. Through the power of total and unconditional selfLove, you can recognize your body's perfect health, and once acknowledged, the body will reflect that creation and be in a purely healthful state. Your physical body will always communicate with you about how you love yourSelf. If you choose to abuse your body, it will reflect the side-effects of that abuse. In selfLove, we make choices that honor us in all ways, and through such choices, we maintain powerful physical health.

Your body is the direct reflection of how you love yourSelf. It reflects your emotional status, as well as your belief system and self-image. Why is acne suffered almost solely by teenagers? They may have a fear of facing situations in their lives, or perhaps have difficulty putting their "best face forward," or perhaps are afraid to face their futures.

Interestingly, when a person sees a pimple on his or her face, do they notice the perfection of the rest of the skin? By focusing on the pimple with frustration, pain and judgment, he puts forth an energetic body language which prompts more pimples to appear. The body will always respond to the root emotion receiving our concentration. Therefore, it is important to focus on those parts of the body that bring you peace, as in this case, clear skin. By ignoring the clarity of your skin, you are communicating to your body that clear skin does not get your attention, so it will create a means to have you pay attention to its needs.

When one is suffering from depression, the entire body reflects that energy by shutting down. Depression creates the slowing down of movement, both physically and energetically. A depressed person needs more sleep because the body functions slow down. The body is responding to the choice to hold so much emotional pain that the person is becoming the pain and shutting down. It is the root of the pain which must be released for the total healing to take place. Medication simply covers up the symptoms, and the body will reflect the depression in other ways at another time.

When a woman is dealing with sexual issues, in many cases she gains weight in order to cover up her sexuality, due to an unconscious choice to be undesirable to men. This occurs in many rape situations. Other reasons for weight gain or loss involve control issues. When one believes that one is out of control, the body simply reflects that energy through insatiable appetite or total lack of desire to eat. Both of these phenomena are the reflection of a person's belief that they have no control over their own lives.

When dealing with a physical challenge, call the entire body forth to do the healing. The body has a consciousness of the oneness of its Being. Therefore, if you stub your toe, have your whole body participate in its healing. Simply talk to your body. Request that it remove the pain and ask that it quickly bring balance and harmony to the pained toe. Your body will respond to your request, and the pain will surely be released within a short period of time.

Sophie* came to me with a number of complaints, not the least among them being the arthritic pain and deformity she was struggling with in her hands. In sharing her history, Sophie discussed the fact that both of her parents were deaf, and the emotional difficulties this presented to her in her years growing up.

What I was able to determine from her story was that Sophie was holding much anger in her hands, which were her tools of communication with her parents via sign language. She had agonized over being different from her friends, particularly during the difficult adolescent years. This energy of anger was held within the cellular memory of her hands, and, as she grew older, it manifested into self-created illness. Arthritis did not manifest anywhere else in her body, and once Sophie made the choice to release the anger and shame of her youth, she was able to invite her body to release the energies which created the disharmony in her hands.

Our bodies will always be a mirror of our thoughts, our beliefs, our self-image. If we look critically at ourSelves and do not like an image we see with our eyes, then that image grows, and we will see only that which we focus upon. It is of great importance that we focus our energies upon that which we love about ourSelves in every aspect of our Being, thus allowing the parts of us we love to become the focus of our energy, which then permits this aspect to grow.

Once we choose to see perfection in our bodies, then our bodies resonate in that energy of perfection. This comes when we experience total selfLove. No matter what body shape or size, if you can gaze at the reflection of your body in the mirror and truly love yourSelf in that shape, you are on the road to creating the body image you most desire. If your body carries an illness within and you fully embrace yourSelf in selfLove, the illness will more easily be healed, because of the body's reflection of that love.

We are all God. As God, we have the power to create the bodies of our choosing. As God, we can imagine ourSelves to be whatever we want to be. We can allow the years to pass without buying into the aging process. We are bombarded with information warning us what to expect at this stage of life or that stage of life. We limit ourSelves because of belief systems others force upon us, but we truly have the power to overcome stimuli and create for ourSelves the perfection that we deserve to be!

In loving our bodies, it is essential to feed our bodies appropriate nutrition and to allow our bodies a release of pent-up energies through exercise. We cannot ignore basic truths about the fuel we need. Different elements of all food groups create the building blocks to perfect health. Conversely, some foods deplete energy and create a burden on different organ systems of our bodies. This is not to say that we can never eat a chocolate bar or have a beer. Rather, all things should be enjoyed in moderation. If one is a caffeine addict, restrict yourSelf to no more than two cups of coffee (or other caffeinated product) per day. Drink a lot of water to wash through impurities. Have as little refined sugar as possible without depriving yourSelf of the joy of eating. If you crave sweets, eat more fruit. If you need to chew, reach for crisp vegetables. Skip all soda and drink purified water. Treat yourSelf occasionally (in moderation!) and be sure to make more high-fiber and low-fat choices.

Before you choose what you eat, ask your body what it wants. It will answer you! Begin by hydrating with a glass of water. Then simply imagine the food. Place your hands open-palmed over your solar-plexus and ask your body if this food will honor you. Your body will begin to sway backwards or forwards. If your body goes back, it is pushing you away from this food choice; if your body moves forward, it embraces that choice! Learn to communicate with your physical body. It has a total consciousness and always wants what is best for itself...and for you!

Exercise need not be a burden. As little as ten minutes each day can bring tremendous change. Love yourSelf enough to honor your body. Strengthen your immune system, drain your lymphatic system, increase your blood circulation and get those organs humming along by simply stepping up an activity to the point of

Do a nutritional analysis of how you are presently honoring your body:

Do you drink coffee, soda or alcohol?

Do you drink at least 8 glasses of purified water daily?

Do you start each day with a good breakfast?

Do you have more than one serving of a refined sugar product daily?

Do you eat close to 3 fruits and 4 vegetables daily?

Do you eat fish twice per week?

Do you take vitamin supplements?

Look at your answers. How are you loving your body?

bringing your respiration level up and filling your lungs with much-needed air! Exercise should be a part of the day equal to brushing your teeth, something you choose to do simply to maintain perfection and prevent decay!

Honor the miracle of your body, regardless of your personal experience in this moment. Whether you are experiencing perfect health or dealing with health challenges, honor the wholeness of your Being, and recognize that, if you focus on that which you do not have, you will not achieve it. In other words, if you focus on illness rather than health, weakness rather than strength, and even if you focus on weight issues or wrinkles or any other lack, that is what you are creating, through thought, upon the physical. Love yourSelf. Love your body. It is the experience of who you are in this moment...and if you want to change it, then change it by falling in love with you!

— OUR MINDS —

Thoughts are all-important to our state of Being. You are what you think. What do you think of yourSelf? How do you "see" yourSelf? If you are ill, where is your focus—on your healing or on your illness? Do you take responsibility for your thoughts? Your feelings?

We create our experiences. Experiment with it! Spend a week focusing one hundred percent of your thoughts on loving and accepting all that you are. Always see the silver lining in the cloud. Create each moment of each day, anticipating only joyful experiences. Send loving thoughts to everyone you meet; reach out and touch the heart of another with love from your own. Expect wondrous things, and then step aside and allow them to become your reality!

All healing begins in the heart, but acceptance must partner with your mind and your thoughts. Emotional baggage honors limitation and pain, thereby creating illness-related experiences. Make the choice to honor yourSelf and find the path to clearing away this energy of emotion—your rage, your frustration, your hate, your fear, your grief, your guilt. Not necessarily an easy task, but truly a simple shift. It will take time and commitment, but ultimately the choice is your own. You have the power, as God, to choose to love yourSelf differently. As you change, so do the expressions of your world and the experiences of your life!

Belief systems create the reality of our lives. I know a man who lost over a hundred-and-fifty pounds and brought himSelf to a perfect size for his height. However, he always "saw" himSelf as heavy, and his belief system created an energy that made him appear heavier than he was to others. Ultimately, he struggled with maintaining his new weight, simply because he couldn't accept himSelf. His belief system worked against the physical reality of his changed body and put forth energy to recreate his obesity.

I have worked with women who are dealing with challenges regarding breast cancer. In fact, Rose* called me to discuss healing at the request of a friend, because she was contemplating the double mastectomy of her two healthy breasts. Her mother, aunt and sister had all suffered and died of breast cancer, and she wanted to avoid this experience in her life.

I challenged her belief that she would ultimately be a victim of this disease, simply because those around her had created it for themSelves. Rose truly thought that the odds were against her, and I was unable to move her belief system to one of a more powerful and positive creation. She was so insistent that this was to be that I knew in my heart that this would become her creation.

Sadly, many women deal with this same belief. Another woman, Maggie*, lost her mother to breast cancer, and from that moment forward, she talked

List your top three beliefs about your body.

Are these beliefs of love and acceptance or of pain?

How can you choose differently?

about the powerful possibility that it would happen to her, as well. She strongly embraced this energy, and sadly, after carrying this belief for thirteen years, she created the need for a mastectomy.

On the other hand, many women are refusing to accept the medical paradigm that cancer runs in the family. Almost all families have cancer! It is not just genes that bring about cancer; it is also self-hatred and fear. There is a direct emotional link to cancer, depending upon where in the body this creation is manifested. People who feel powerless create illness in the reproductive organs; lung cancer is developed when one is suffocating in an aspect of their lives; colon cancer is rooted in the body when a person lives his life holding back words or feelings, or in people who "stuff" down their emotions; liver cancer is the result of undeniable rage. Each organ system can be linked to an emotional reality created in the mind and belief of the person. When you take responsibility for how you feel, you can then release these emotions and free yourSelf from this destructive pathway.

Visualization is a powerful healing tool, allowing thought to partner with desire, thereby creating a new reality. As we acknowledge our ability to heal, we create the energy needed to bring about change and move our body into this new creation of health.

It is important to recognize that, through visualization, we are simply choosing, as God, what the outcome will be. Visualizing an army of beings attacking a cancerous tumor is creating the energy the body needs to rally and fight off the cells which have been running amuck. Visualizing laser beams of light attacking a tumor is equally potent, allowing energy and vibrational shifts to create a disharmony within the tumor itself, causing physical changes within.

The power of visualization should come as no surprise. A woman who sees her hands as the most beautiful part of her body will take great pains to care for them. She will have weekly manicures and use lotions to keep her skin soft. This attention is real, yet the energy of beauty in her hands comes from her visualization. So powerful is her belief that, indeed, as the years progress, her hands will stay youthful and lovely.

We should always choose to see ourSelves as perfect, for we are. Through selfLove we can free ourSelves of all pain and lack. We can always visualize ourSelves as we want to see ourSelves to be, knowing fundamentally that however we are is perfect, and that wanting to experience a change is equally perfect. We should look at our reflection in the mirror and focus on the aspects of our bodies that we love. We can let go of fear each time we feel a weakness in our muscles; rather, we can choose always to remember to thank our bodies for being so magnificent and perfect, and guide our thoughts to honor this perfection.

If we live in fear, we will create fearful experiences in our lives. If we seek attention through illness, we will create an illness so tenacious that we will ultimately create an irreversible situation, simply through thought. If we focus on the ills of the body, the body will create more ills to capture the energy of that focus.

Releasing fear is necessary in order to achieve total healing. Loving oneSelf is the opposite energy of that based in fear. We will all heal through love, once we accept and choose to experience total love for Self. And to love yourSelf is the greatest gift you can give to yourSelf and to everyone around you. For, as you love yourSelf, you have all the more love to share.

— OUR SPIRITS —

There are a great many people all over the globe who are experiencing more than simply the physical nature of life. They are touching upon an inner aspect of connection to the energies of life all around them. As spiritual expansion continues throughout the world, more people will choose to awaken to a greater level of understanding regarding who we are.

More books on different aspects of spirituality are being written...and read. The New Age movement is a magnificent reflection of the shift of energy from left brain to right brain, accessing levels of knowing which go far beyond what we have ever been taught. Whenever one seeks spiritual information, it is imperative that it *feel* good within the heart of the seeker. It matters not who the teacher is, for all of us are teachers and students. We all learn from one another.

In the quest for healing, many spiritual seekers reach out to non-Western healing modalities. Many of these modalities involve energetic work, accessing levels of spiritual knowing without physical tools. The only tool needed in healing is love. Whether a person uses a piece of equipment or works with crystals or beads or other such creations, it is their connection to their love of Self which will make them as powerful as they choose to be, in order to bring healing to the heart of another.

In healing, all begins within one's heart. When your heart heals, your body will heal as well. Without working through heart energy, the healing of the physical is temporary at best. The spiritual aspect of Being is the center of one's life. The soul should be touched upon, so that the body may finally allow the release of the illness creation.

In my personal experience, I have come to realize that many spiritual seekers pick and choose what they wish to embrace in their spiritual lives. This cannot be. I am always surprised when a person speaks "Spiritualese" within their powerful walls of self-limitation. So many people know the pat phrases and flash them around, yet they are not committed to the truth within those very words! For instance, many will discuss *karma* (past lifetimes' choices creating this lifetime's obligations and experiences) and *soul choices* (prior to our birth, our souls each choose the lessons which must be learned in this lifetime). This New Age conversation simply reflects one's unwillingness to take responsibility for choices made in each moment of *now!*

What we need to understand is that our essence—our "soul" body—is simply us as pure love. In the physical, we can choose to allow this love to inhabit our choices...as joy or as pain. We can choose to take responsibility for our lives and let go of beliefs which cast blame elsewhere.

Think about the language you use to describe why things are the way they are in your life.

Do you say "the universe" or "God" will provide? Do you say, "What I do for others will come back to me?" Do you believe the alignment of the stars or energy fields determines your experiences? Do you always "put it out there" and then wait for something to come to you?

Are you ready to take responsibility for the circumstances of your life?

And so, as we live in difficult relationships, or have traumatic life experiences involving another, we can accept the responsibility for our choices and release the need to make excuses for these experiences as though we have no power. We are God and make choices in all moments and in all ways. We cannot pick and choose that which we label as karma and that which we do not.

In my working with Jeanne*, a victim of horrible childhood abuse which truly goes beyond belief, I discovered a woman of incredible intellect and empowerment. Jeanne spent many years working through the trauma of her early life. During those years, she studied the work of many spiritual teachers and read great quantities of spiritual writings. Jeanne could quote to perfection works from the great masters and from the Bible, and through these studies, she embraced the hugeness of her life. However, when challenged with the possibility that she *chose* this life's experience of abuse, she always responded in horror and rage, refusing to be held responsible for her victimization.

Jeanne was unable to separate herSelf from her feelings of helpless victimization. She did not want to acknowledge that, as a child suffering such torment at the hands of her father, she came as a very powerful teacher. Jeanne rejected this truth and decided that it did not apply to her situation. She viewed the level of her abuse as one that went beyond the choice to teach her father how to choose love for himSelf, rather than his personal pain. She argued that, if her soul did indeed choose this path, it would not have chosen such extreme pain. "How could it?" she would ask.

By doing this, Jeanne was able to lay the blame of her experience fully upon her perpetrator, rather than accepting the perfection of her choice to teach her father love. Until Jeanne chooses acceptance and release, she will not be fully healed. She may function well, but she will always maintain energies which will prevent her from living in total selfLove.

We should never choose to diminish the experience of another. We can choose to always honor another's choice, no matter what we see for them that they cannot see for themSelves. In the case of Jeanne, the healing continues. There are great lessons to be shared here. In our work, I always honor her belief structure, and we continue to take steps together towards the final release of energy which will free her to fully experience her magnificence. She will come to know herSelf at the soul level, once she accepts her truth.

Our Spirit is a living energy. It is as real as the physical body. It is our essential experience of Self. Everything we experience is simply the manifestation of this living energy. We should honor our soul; it should be loved, respected and cared for daily. What we perceive to be the physical is simply the illusion and reflection of our perceptions, and the spirit is the heart of who we truly are. Nothing sustains the physical except selfLove. As we honor the love that we are, all other aspects of Self vibrate in this experience of selfLove, and the healing is profound.

You can choose to give your soul freedom to express itself fully in all moments. You can learn to quiet your mind long enough to be able to hear the whispers of your soul. In meditation, the messages always come from within. Psychics can tap into the collective energies of All, allowing for conscious knowing and access of information; however, the knowing will always come from your own heart.

It is important to make time to be in silence with Self, for it is here in the silence that our spirit can find its voice and be heard. When facing a healing crisis, this quiet space allows for greater communication between spirit and body. We each have great knowing and can choose to make the time and take the opportunity to access this knowing. Illness is your soul's way of getting your attention, communicating valuable information to you about how you are choosing to love yourSelf.

Illness is created energetically before it reaches the physical body. Therefore, as we learn to listen to the whispers of our souls, we can uncover energetic blocks which may lead to physical illness. Listen with an open heart and with acceptance, and you will learn the root of the dis-ease. Once you know what it is, you can then move into your healing experience.

Meditation is an appropriate healing tool, since it closes down abstract thought and allows for the knowing to flow in greater peace. Many people claim they cannot quiet their minds long enough to receive information. This becomes their reality, simply because they believe it so strongly. Every person has the ability to be in silence; it is nothing more than choosing to do so. It may take time and practice, but it is always possible.

If one is ill and meditation is prescribed, the desire is greater, and often that person is capable of experiencing silence. Why wait until illness strikes? Avoid challenges of the body, mind or emotional aspects of Self by creating a peaceful energy around yourSelf by choosing a life that is joyful for you. Honor your spiritual Being. It carries great knowing of who you are. Listen to your knowing with an open heart and thoughtless mind, and your personal world will find peace and harmony.

CHAPTER FIFTEEN

The Five Stages of Healing

*We create illness, not because we do **not** love ourselves, but because of **how** we do—with neglect, disappointment, judgment and self-hate.*

It is of great importance to recognize that, although healing can be profound, it takes time for the physical body to "catch up" to the energetic healing experienced through selfLove. Many of my clients end our session feeling changed, but each then has the responsibility of continuing to make choices in selfLove for quite some time before the body comes to a full response of total healing. The responsibility is ultimately theirs; each person is given "homework," which continues to support the healing. To imagine that a person who facilitates healing has the magic cure is unrealistic; it has taken many years to create the physical challenge, and so it will take time to change it.

Early in the book, I introduced Jane*, a woman diagnosed with inoperable lung cancer. It would have been natural for Jane to wish for a miraculous change in her body, especially after hearing the dreadful verdict presented to her. As do many clients, Jane came to me in great fear. This is a natural reaction for all of us when facing a challenging illness and needing assistance, whether from a medical professional or an alternative practitioner. Fear is a manifestation of vulnerability; when people seek healing, they feel extremely vulnerable and powerless. The first and most important gift I give back to each client is their power, for, in acknowledging their power, they can take the reins of their own healing.

It takes much work to regain and then maintain this power. It is important for each client to be in control. In Jane's case, she was asked to do color breath-work, meditation and visualizations. Needless to say, she did everything she could, with great belief in the final outcome of total healing. These energies charged her body with a renewed sense of vitality and self-empowerment.

Jane is now free and clear of her illness, but it took months of work, filled with moments of setbacks. She had many emotions which made her feel as if she were on a roller-coaster ride. The "down" periods never superseded her hard work, for she simply accepted her moments of fear and depression, let them pass, and then resumed the work at hand with heightened expectations.

Jane's healing is perhaps a miracle, but it occurred due to her persistence and commitment to herSelf and the acceptance of her own selfLove.

There are five stages each person goes through to allow healing. They are Acceptance, Acknowledgment, Honoring, Choice and Being. These stages represent the choices that must be honored, if great changes are to occur in all aspects of Self— physical, mental, emotional, cellular, spiritual and energetic. One need not be aware of the particular stage one is in, but I have observed that, as the flow from one stage to the next takes place, the healing experience becomes more and more definitive in one's personal creation.

Regardless of the method people choose to use in order to heal, if they do not move through these five stages, healing will perhaps take place, but only temporarily. As each item is discussed specifically, it will make sense to see that, without *Acceptance* of responsibility for all as one's creation; without *Acknowledgment* of their truth as it is; without *Honoring* their choices as perfect rather than holding on to them with limitation, separation and pain; without *Choosing* to heal by loving Self in all moments, there will be no change; and finally, by allowing themSelves to experience Self in perfection, they can *Be* all that they are.

I once worked with an older gentleman, Fred*, who contacted me because he had been suffering from a variety of physical ailments for most of his life. He was frustrating to work with, because he was in such a powerful state of denial about his life, his choices and his reality that he would not even listen to anything I shared with him. He spent almost every moment of our conversation complaining over and over again about his childhood, which had been difficult. Having been sent from orphanage to orphanage as a young boy, Fred kept telling me that he was never nurtured, and that this was the root of his issues in this lifetime.

Fred was already in his seventies. Sadly, he never moved out of the rage created by his childhood. He was ill and friendless, unable to understand why people did not like him. He went from therapist to therapist, because each one told him they couldn't help him. I, too, had to let this client go, because he was unwilling—but never *unable*—to make changes in the way he thought, spoke or behaved.

Fred refused to accept responsibility for his life experience as the manifestation of his choices. When I challenged him about loving himSelf, he claimed that he did and listed endless reasons to prove it. His lack of selfLove was powerfully evident to everyone he had ever worked with, and yet he would not acknowledge this basic truth. Fred could not imagine that his behavior reflected his lack of selfLove, because if he had done so, he would have had to face the reality that no one loved him, and this was too difficult.

Sometimes we choose to learn through pain. It is just another way to learn. Acknowledgment of the core issue, the second stage of healing, remained hidden from Fred's consciousness. He was in such denial that he could not allow any shred of truth to enter his thoughts. Without accepting one's own reality and creation of dis-ease, how can one heal?

Fred refused to see his perfection or the perfection of his life. At all moments, we have pathways of choice. We have the freedom to choose different expressions of existence, which enable us to change our reality based upon experiences we have brought into our lives. All is in perfection, and each experience offers opportunity to learn, grow and change.

Fred remained so strongly "stuck" in his childhood memories and issues of abandonment that he was still experiencing abandonment through his therapists and others with whom he hoped to work. Fred did not honor himSelf, and so, who else could? Nor would he commit to any of the healing plans offered to him over the years by a large number of medical and holistic practitioners. Fred simply wanted his life changed without committing to the partnership necessary to create these changes!

Finally, not only did Fred not believe that he was God and therefore powerful, but he had no belief in God at all. After all, how could God abandon a child the way he had been abandoned? The way Fred looked at his life, if there was a God, Fred would have had a happy family. Fred blamed his life on every other player outside of himSelf, and he carried throughout his life much misery and loneliness.

Fred is an example of passive creation. Once Fred became a young man, he had many opportunities to build a full life for himSelf. He could have chosen to ignore his past, not deal with it emotionally and move into total denial, as many people do. This would indeed have created health challenges in later years, but at least his life would have been full and productive. Or else, in his younger years, he could have chosen to deal with his issues by seeking therapy, thus ridding himSelf of his pain and from there building a healthy new creation.

Fred's childhood was what it was, but Fred chose to hold on to his vision of a perfect childhood, living in resentment of what he had not experienced. Because of this choice to hold on to his pain, Fred never spent a moment living. He only spent his time remembering. And so, he never moved past his pain, allowing this pain to be his only creation.

Healing requires commitment...to Self. Illness is a powerful creation, which is simply the body's way of calling attention to issues it has been dealing with at energetic and cellular levels. What begins emotionally slowly moves into the physical structure of one's Being. One should not ignore any powerful emotional experience, for this energy will always find a way to settle within the body, unless resolution comes with equal passion and total truth.

You cannot fool your body, although you can fool yourSelf into believing that you have released the discord of your experience. And when the body offers you physical proof that the discord still exists, you can choose to accept this truth and love yourSelf enough to partner with your body to accomplish total healing.

— ACCEPTANCE —

The first stage of healing is *acceptance of Self as perfect*—even your pain, be it emotional, mental, psychological or physical. Acceptance comes through selfLove. When we fully love ourSelves, we understand that nothing in our lives exists without our full participation. Every experience we call forth through thought, word or action is a perfect opportunity to recognize how we love ourSelves, since everything that is, is an expression of love.

When we call forth illness, we are simply telling ourSelves that we have been choosing limitation and pain as an expression of the love that we are. Illness offers us the opportunity to learn and to choose to make the changes needed to love Self...and thereby begin to heal.

It is often difficult for people to admit that they could possibly create any ailment they are dealing with. It is easier to blame illness on the environment or on the emotions experienced through interactions with others. No one causes your emotions; you are solely responsible for your feelings and reactions towards others. If you have difficulty with another person in your life, you have the freedom to make the changes needed to honor yourSelf. If you choose not to make these changes, then the responsibility lies with you.

Today, people are bringing lawsuits against the tobacco industry, blaming tobacco companies for creating their illnesses, even though they personally made the choice to smoke cigarettes. Although it is perhaps true that when they began to smoke years ago, some people didn't know that it would be addictive or life-threatening, the fact is that this truth has been publicly known for many decades.

Many people have taken the more challenging road of stopping smoking, battling their nicotine addiction and suffering the side effects. In each instance, this act was made in powerful selfLove, allowing the physical body to resume its natural healing path.

Those who choose to continue to smoke and blame the ill effects on others or the industry are not accepting responsibility for their own actions. Should the tobacco industry be held responsible for one's personal choice? Why do some people choose differently from others? Why are some people more successful than others in quitting this addiction? It all comes down to how each person chooses to experience life.

Accepting the perfection of your experience of illness is the first step towards recognizing that the disease is perfect, as a manifestation of how you are loving yourSelf. Only then can one move into the next phases of healing. And it is more than simply speaking the words; it is taking the steps necessary to create the energy behind this acceptance.

Using mySelf as an example, when I discovered that my illness was a cancer that needed to be powerfully and quickly released through surgery and chemotherapy, I became quite depressed. I could not accept this creation and did not understand in what way I was not living in selfLove. I struggled to find the perfection in needing to undergo this entire experience, seeking within my heart the lesson I needed to learn.

I couldn't blame the circumstances of my illness on my environment, for I ate well and cared for my body. I chose not to blame my illness on those outside of me, because I recognized my responsibility for my own creations.

I struggled to see the perfection of the moment, while filled with fear, grief and shame. But as I continued to work through the experience, I began to reflect on my own lack of selfLove by listening to my words and watching my choices more carefully. With purposeful choices and the loving but honest assistance of friends and family, I awakened to my own lack of selfLove and began to choose differently in my life.

The perfection of this experience is simply that the illness allowed me to recognize that I was not living in selfLove. As I made choices to love mySelf in all moments through thoughts, words and actions, the healing became profound.

Understanding the perfection of each experience is the most powerful step towards total healing. Many clients claim, when asked, that they do, indeed, love themSelves. I then ask them, as limitless Beings, what the illness is trying to tell them about how they are limiting themselves...how they are *loving* themselves?

So what exactly is selfLove? *It is the celebration of Self in all moments.* SelfLove is an experience of Being, in which you recognize the perfection of who you are. It is the acknowledgment of your magnificence. It is the acceptance of Self and all others without judgment. It is the acceptance of the experience of choices made in pain or fear as being equal to those made in love and joy, for, in each moment, we create as God and experience that which we bring forth without judgment of greater or lesser, better or worse.

When illness is created, it is an experience we bring forth in order to allow us to choose differently and change our lives. All experiences are of love. We create illness, not because we do *not* love ourSelves, but because of *how* we do—with neglect, disappointment, judgment and self-hate. Illness is a manifestation of how we love ourSelves, a reminder that we need to explore selfLove more fully, and an opportunity to choose how to change our lives, so that we may experience peace in our hearts.

Once we release the limitation of our own love, the illness has no reason to continue to be our teacher. Our bodies have no desire to create disharmony in our lives; the disharmony is simply the body's way of getting our attention. Once we recognize symptoms of disharmony, we can get to the root of the creation by recognizing where we lost sight of our magnificent state of Being.

Illness is an opportunity for each of us to learn great lessons...and this process can always enhance our experience of selfLove.

Stephanie* was the victim of much abuse as a child, in all aspects of Being. She endured sexual abuse, as well as psychological and physical abuse. Having gone through many years of therapy, Stephanie was now embracing spirituality as a means of finding peace in her heart. She shared with many friends the great spiritual lessons she had learned, but, interestingly, never fully embraced these lessons herSelf. Asked if she loved herSelf, she was honest in admitting that she did not. She reflected upon her childhood, allowing her memories of being told that she was unlovable to be carried forward into adulthood.

Stephanie had difficulty taking responsibility for present-day choices, using her childhood experiences as excuses for many of her actions. She hoarded every piece of paper that crossed her path, creating havoc in her small apartment. She was unable to let anything go, saying that this was because, as a child, she had always needed to prove her actions to her parents. By holding on to all those scraps of paper, she always had proof with which she could defend herSelf. Yet, in conversation, Stephanie demonstrated great understanding of her creation and self-limitation.

By holding onto the beliefs of her youth, Stephanie felt unlovable. Although she knew that she chose the experiences of her childhood, even understanding that these experiences had been created to teach her great lessons, Stephanie was unwilling to recognize her magnificence. She had difficulty receiving gifts, but was free in offering gifts to others. She felt unworthy, telling me that she recognized her responsibility to make changes in her personal world, but was unwilling to take that step toward healing.

For Stephanie, the healing process was more difficult than necessary, because she was challenged by her fear of letting go of her pain. However, over time, she has improved greatly. Someday, she may choose to release, through choice, the blocks created long ago. She will embrace the lessons she so lovingly shares with others and will recognize her power to create the magnificence of her future.

Another client, Maggie*, had no physical ailments but called me to discuss matters of the heart. She was lonely and alone and wanted to know why she was unsuccessful in her personal relationships with men. She wanted nothing more than a healthy relationship that could lead to marriage and a family, and yet she was energetically creating the exact opposite in her life.

I explained to Maggie that she first had to choose to love herSelf, in order to create the energy that would enable her to share love with others. This perception was frustrating to Maggie, because she perceived herSelf as a loving person and one who loved herSelf deeply. After all, did she not do everything she wanted to do and buy herSelf everything she wanted to have and go to all the places she wanted to visit? When I challenged her on this definition of selfLove, Maggie had difficulty acknowledging this truth about herSelf. I told her that, when she would be in joy with who she was—alone but not lonely—then things would change in her life.

Maggie had difficulty accepting herSelf and her life as perfect. She was always looking over her shoulder at the joy she perceived in others and, rather than celebrating that joy, going into a state of envy. Maggie was always thinking, "Why them and not me?" which eliminated her understanding of the power of her own creations.

She never fully released her childhood issues. Having been raised in an overprotective household, she chose to free herSelf from her family by separating herSelf emotionally from them. It was this choice that separated Maggie emotionally from *all* people, and this is what kept her from establishing close relationships in her adult life.

When we accept Self as perfect, we open our hearts to the opportunity of understanding who we are in all moments. We also understand that, if *we* are perfect, then *All* are perfect. No one is greater or lesser than another; no experience is judged "good" or "bad." It simply is. And by letting it be what it is, we can look at it from a neutral vantage point. Neutrality enables us to accept the choice that brought us to that experience, thus allowing us to recognize what we can change in order to bring forth a different experience.

Illness is an experience of Being. If you do not want to experience your illness, accept the perfection of it and make the necessary changes that will allow you to learn through choices which come from selfLove.

— Acknowledgement —

The New Age movement embraces a great many holistic and alternative healing practices. Part of the language of the movement suggests that each person carries their own "truth" within themSelves, and that each person is entitled to their own "truth." Many of my clients tell me that *their* "truth" is different from the energy which I perceive to be at the root of the emotional issues creating their illness, that they are finished with the issue at hand and have moved past that point in their personal evolution.

Naturally, if this were the case, their bodies would not carry the reflection of the disharmony created by the root emotions. In many instances, I spend much time speaking with clients, explaining that there is no "your truth" and "my truth," but only one Truth that exists for all in each moment. This Truth is the acknowledgment that we each are God, and, as such, have the power to create through choice all the experiences of our lives.

It is challenging to believe that you are God. We have been taught otherwise for thousands of years. God has been described in a myriad of ways. People who have released religious limitations see God as a "spark within" or a "divine energy" that we are all part of. This definition, too, creates limitation for Self. We are whole and perfect in all moments. We are powerful and magnificent. We are responsible for our experiences through our thoughts, words and actions. We are God—creators of our lives in all moments.

It is also challenging for many to acknowledge their choice, as God, to create the pain that called forth the illness, whether it be physical or emotional. It is difficult for clients to accept that they are ill because they are unhappy in the lives they have created. They go into powerful denial, simply because they do not wish to deal with the issues they would have to face in order to heal. Sometimes, for example, a person may have to consider getting a divorce in order to create the freedom necessary for total healing. Sometimes a relationship with a parent would have to be changed. There have been times when job stress is the root of illness-creation, and the fear of changing one's employment situation becomes greater than the desire to heal. The bottom line is simply that each of us can choose to step back and look at our own behaviors, and then acknowledge the truth that we created our situation because of our own personal choices.

I have known Donna* for many years. She is a very happy and loving woman, who refuses to acknowledge her truth. She is quite successful in her business, but outside of her work environment, Donna diminshes herSelf.

It is fascinating to watch Donna create her world. In business, she exudes knowledge, confidence and power, thus attracting clients to her like a magnet. However, in her personal life, Donna is afraid and insecure. She does not acknowledge her power as God in her personal life. Once Donna acknowledges the limitations and lack she creates in her personal life, she will choose differently, thus allowing the empowered Self she expresses through her business choices to permeate her personal world.

However, Donna argues this issue quite profoundly, telling me that *her* truth is different from my perception of it. She does not acknowledge that she has chosen that certain parts of her life be lacking. When I ask her if she is in total joy in all aspects of her life, she can show enthusiasm only in discussing her work. At a deeper level, she is aware of her unhappiness, but she is afraid to go into her truth and therefore cannot acknowledge her self-created limitations.

We are powerful Beings, yet we limit our power through our fears. Once we embrace the knowing that we are God, we can change any aspect of life, if we choose to do so; but first, we should fully and powerfully know what our choices are, and, to discern this, we must face our fears and move into total truth.

Jonathan* was facing challenges, rooted in fear, that prevented him from embracing his full career potential. He had reached a roadblock in his career and recognized that he had been too comfortable for too long in a position he enjoyed. Because of his fun personality and light-hearted manner, he was loved by his staff and fellow employees, but he was rarely offered opportunities leading towards advancement within the ranks of his company. Jonathan was a wonderful husband and father and quite contented in his life, within the limitations of his own making. He was torn between comfortably staying where he was or expanding his experience and reaching into the unknown.

Interestingly, Jonathan was approached by a competitor of his current employer, who offered him an opportunity to interview for a highly visible position in their company. The day before this interview, I worked with Jonathan. Together, we uncovered his core issue: throughout his school days and early career, his family had protected him from possible failures. Jonathan never stretched to reach for the stars. He was treated like a king, regardless of choices that had kept him from reaching his fullest potential. In fact, his parents tried to dissuade Jonathan from even having this interview, worrying that, should he fail, he would become despondent. Jonathan's parents wanted to protect their son from the pain of failure.

I showed Jonathan that, as a result of this upbringing, it was natural that he always expected to fail, since he had not allowed himSelf the freedom to experience disappointment or even success in reaching beyond the guaranteed achievements of his life.

Once Jonathan embraced this truth, he was ready to fly. Not only did he receive a job offer on the day of the interview, which is unusual in such a high management position, but his current employer, when faced with his resignation, made Jonathan a lucrative counter-offer which he had long deserved. Jonathan began to see his entire life from the vantage point of success rather than failure. Once he uncovered this truth, he was happy to release the limitations created by this truth and was then free to fly into the glorious expansion of his world.

Discovering and acknowledging your truth can be challenging, because it brings up painful issues long-buried within your heart. You will experience selfLove when you are willing to recognize the truth of your limitations and acknowledge your choice in embracing them. It is too easy to blame your idiosyncrasies on your childhood, flippantly using this as an excuse for behaviors expressed in your adult life. And you cannot blame others around you for the life you are living, for there are always choices which can be made towards creating the changes you desire. The responsibility for your life is your own; it takes but a thought or action to begin to change life as it is and to discover the life you have always wanted to experience.

Acknowledge that you are God. Acknowledge that all you have experienced in your life has been the result of your choices as God. Acknowledge the truth of who you are, and you will experience greater peace in body, mind and spirit. Your heart will sing with joy and empowerment, and you will resonate at every level with the energy of You!

— HONORING —

SelfLove is experienced when we honor all that we are. As we choose to celebrate everything that we are in all moments, we acknowledge the perfection of Self. If we wish to release an aspect of Self we no longer choose to experience, we do not fully let it go until we embrace it with love. As we honor all that we are, we love all that we are. As we honor illness as an experience we brought forth through our own choices, we allow ourSelves the opportunity to learn through this choice, love the choice and release it. What follows is the physical manifestation of healing.

Each person has the freedom and ability to look upon who they are and honor what they see. If we judge ourSelves, we can choose to release our judgments about aspects of ourSelves that we do not love. All that we are exists as the result of prior choices. Allow yourSelf the joy of loving ALL that you are. Stop criticizing and judging, and instead learn to accept, allow and choose to change or let it be...and discover peace.

We should honor Self, releasing the choice to live in comparison to another, or to an ideal created by our society. We can choose to change what we have previously created by honoring our prior choices, loving them and letting them go, then replacing them with new choices created with love. We can choose to express appreciation for the aspects of Self we enjoy, be it the suppleness of our muscles, the smoothness of our skin, the thickness of our hair, the brightness of our eyes. As we honor that which we admire about ourSelves, we slowly begin to discover more attributes of which we were previously unaware. Our attention becomes directed towards the positive rather than the negative, and this becomes an overall pattern in all aspects of our lives.

As we honor our physical body, it automatically begins to respond with corresponding energy. We can always communicate with the body's consciousness and make choices that will enhance the experience of our perfection.

Our oldest daughter Jodi was preparing for a two-month visit to Nepal, during which time she was planning a trek of three weeks or more into the Himalayas. At five-feet-three and only 115 pounds, Jodi is petite. She recognized the need to prepare for the trek and began a program of swimming each morning before work to tone her muscles. As the weather warmed, she changed her exercise routine and began hiking the Colorado trails to build stamina. Gradually, she began to hike with more and more weight in her backpack, since she was planning to trek without the assistance of a porter, who is normally hired to carry the trekkers' bags.

Interestingly, Jodi began to suffer from migraine headaches and nausea on many of her days off, often correlating with days when she'd planned to hike. She was pushing her body to carry 45+ pounds on her back, which was the approximate weight of the supplies she was preparing to take on her journey.

One day, during one of her headaches, I challenged Jodi, asking her if she was communicating with her body. I urged her to ask her body what it wanted and if her choice to carry this weight was honoring her. At that moment, Jodi was too ill to connect to her inner voice, so I advised her to promise her body that she would not force it to work so hard and that she would hire a porter in Nepal. She told her body she would only carry enough food and water for each day's journey, which amounted to approximately fifteen pounds.

Jodi silently spoke to her body's consciousness, and, miraculously, the headache dissipated within three minutes, and she was totally well. She then went into herSelf and listened as her body shared with her its concern that, by creating such powerful physical stress, she would miss out on the spiritual quest she was seeking; that the physical trauma would be a major distraction along this journey of spiritual expansion.

Jodi then admitted to me that, because she was so petite, she wanted to prove to herSelf and others that she was as strong as the larger people around her. She had been choosing a course of action that was not honoring herSelf, but rather one based in ego. As this desire to prove something to someone else was released, her body reacted powerfully in joy and the headaches no longer plagued her.

How we see and honor our perfection will determine our experience. Jodi was always in perfect health but considered her size a limitation, and so she focused her energy and attention upon this self-perceived limitation and created even more of it. Once she honored the perfection of her body and allowed it to guide her choices, her wellness returned, and she was freed of any physical blocks on this path.

I have occasionally guided clients to go into silence for a number of days or weeks, simply to discover their unconditional love for Self. I ask them to do this so that they may learn how to truly honor themSelves. A difficult task, but one which will bring them peace and harmony. When I suggest this to a client, it is usually because I find that a core issue is their need and ultimate choice to always do for others, sacrificing doing for Self.

Earlier, I shared the story of Barbara*, a wonderful person who loved playing a powerful part in the lives of many around her. She truly honored all people and never recognized that her physical ailments were because she had chosen to assist all those who called or visited her. Barbara struggled with a variety of ailments, most of which stemmed from her chronic fatigue syndrome. I found it interesting that Barbara was diagnosed with chronic fatigue, because she always had enough energy for everyone else but never enough for herSelf.

When I asked Barbara to go into silence for a month's time, she was, at first, quite startled. How could she let down everyone around her? What would happen to them if she were not available?

Barbara had to recognize that, by always honoring her friends and family members, she was not honoring herSelf, nor was she being honored by them! It did not take her long to visualize the peace she would enjoy while experiencing her silence. Barbara wrote a few loving letters to her loved ones, expressing her desire to create this separation, and immediately embraced this life-changing experience.

Barbara was allowed to speak, but as little as possible. I advised her never to answer her telephone, and to choose, during this time, activities that honored only herSelf. It was a challenging few weeks, and although Barbara suffered through a natural separation process, by the end of this time, she was stronger and in a state of greatly improved health. Barbara honored herSelf by creating her personal space, and to this day, continues to create boundaries by choosing Self above all, always from selfLove.

We are all perfect just as we are. If we are unhappy with experiences in our lives, we can choose to discover the reasons for these creations and, once discovered, release them. By understanding this truth, we can then agree that even our imperfections are perfect!

Our bodies will always create the energy needed to get our attention. We can choose to honor all aspects of Self. We can love the perfection of who we are—and powerfully honor ourSelves, so that we can move more powerfully into the creation of *Healing Through Love*.

— CHOICE —

To honor oneSelf is simply one's choice. Each moment of each day, we can choose to accept and celebrate who we are. As powerful Beings, we can create, through choice, the existence we want to experience in this and every lifetime.

To live in selfLove, we must choose to love all that we are. Our actions are a direct reflection of how we choose to live. We talk a lot about how we *want* to live, or even about how we *perceive* we are living, but the bottom line is that our actions speak more powerfully than our words. When we live a life of purposeful choice, we *live* that choice, not speak of it.

Many clients with whom I work are concerned with body-image. They have made many choices that have created their experiences, ranging from obesity to anorexia, and the issues are always the same. Food becomes a substance they control in their lives, even when it appears that they are out of control. In fact, it is the rest of their world they think they have no control over, and so they use food to establish a sense of power. It is apparent that, when food is used as a control (or controlling) mechanism, the body is not being honored. Once the person recognizes their personal power, they can release their need to control through food choices and enjoy eating in balanced and healthy moderation.

Body size is a choice—the choice to eat or not, what to eat, and the quantity of food eaten. Too many people claim that they cannot stop themSelves from eating. Of course they can, but they choose not to. How we choose to manifest our bodies is a way to learn about being God. Once we accept our perfection as we are, acknowledge the choices which brought us to this moment and honor these choices through selfLove, we can then choose to change our creations through new and different actions.

Juan* was a young man who spent much of his life dealing with addictive habit patterns: drugs, alcohol, cigarettes and food. He had enough inner resolve to ultimately release his addictions to the drugs, alcohol and cigarettes, but when I met him, he was more than two-hundred pounds overweight. It had taken Juan years to create both the successful end of his earlier addictions and then the resulting obesity, but they were all the reflection of his actions, which were based in his sense of powerlessness. Therefore, it did not matter which addiction he was experiencing; he was still addicted to something outside of himSelf as a way of not embracing his power.

It was extremely difficult for Juan to see his perfection. On the physical level, there was much for the mind to overcome when looking upon the body that was so poorly honored. In his mind, Juan would imagine himSelf two-hundred pounds lighter, but it was difficult for him to maintain that body-image. Spiritually, Juan had the ability to feel the expansiveness of his soul, but he was easily distracted by the body-cravings he had created through his years of self-abuse.

Once Juan would choose to honor himSelf, he would have the strength to make life-changing choices for his physical body. He would have to choose only foods that honored him and drink large quantities of water. Juan lived at home with parents. They, too, were also not living in selfLove, so Juan felt unloved in his immediate environment. His body mass created a wall around him, which was a form of emotional protection, but at the same time created separation between himSelf and most others.

What Juan needed to see within himSelf was what I saw in him—the magnificence of his true Self. Instead, he focused on his flaws. He would choose healthier patterns for a week at a time, but as soon as he had a setback, he would become so frustrated that he would abandon the positive flow. His choice to see himSelf as less than magnificent was more powerful than his desire to heal, and so he continued along the track of dis-ease, which may, in fact, threaten the possibility of his living a long and healthy life.

Lawrence* was an older gentleman who came to me as a last resort. Diagnosed with cirrhosis of the liver, Lawrence had spent the previous two years of his life facing one health challenge after another. As each one was cleared away, both holistically and medically, another challenge would appear.

In telling me his story, Lawrence shared parts of his childhood, which were wrapped in great shame deep within his heart. He had shared his truth with no one, including his wife. Although I was energetically capable of clearing away his current physical situation, I knew that, in order to heal completely and no longer live within the limitation of illness, Lawrence would have to share his story with his family.

As difficult as he knew it would be for him, Lawrence agreed to speak to his wife and adult children, and they all gathered in his home one Sunday afternoon. As he faced them all, he suddenly changed his mind and chose not to discuss his childhood, thereby making a powerful choice not to release the energies creating the serious deterioration of his body. Since he was feeling better from the work we were sharing, he believed that he would heal without having to endure the trauma of sharing his shameful experiences.

What Lawrence did not understand was that his trauma and the shame he was experiencing were at the root of the energy creating his grave deterioration. He believed that, since he felt physically stronger, he would beat his dis-ease. By refusing to partner in his own healing, Lawrence was choosing a shortened lifetime, which would continue to be filled with much suffering.

Of course, for every story of choosing *not* to commit to self-healing, there are so many stories in which people *do* choose to heal! When our paths crossed and she asked for my services, Phyllis* was in a state of depression. Although she was living a limited experience of herSelf, Phyllis chose to change that choice and do all that it would take to heal and flow in joy and perfection.

Together, we created a dietary and nutritional regime which Phyllis chose to embrace fully. As her body became stronger and her spirits continued to rise, she chose to add exercise to her daily routine. Phyllis began to keep a journal listing all of her loving choices, as well as the choices she made that did not honor her as lovingly. She was able to recognize how her choices impacted her life, and she created new ones almost every day. We worked quite closely together, and she was willing to release the blocks she had created in her life. By choosing to embrace her power, Phyllis chose to heal.

Phyllis is a wonderful example of the truth that we all heal ourSelves. I was the facilitator and a witness to her healing process. Her desire was so powerful that this choice alone would have brought her to experience powerful self-healing and expanded knowing. I was watching a butterfly release itself from its cocoon. Phyllis drew on her inner desire and chose to release everything in order to recognize her magnificence. Once in her power, Phyllis began to make new choices for the rest of her life, and to this day continues to act upon them in joy and total selfLove.

Similarly, I worked with an elderly gentleman who came to me struggling with a severe case of psoriasis. Charles* was a man of European roots, educated in the medical field. He was not a powerful believer in holistic practices, but had been unable to find relief through the various doctors he was working with. Once we determined how toxic Charles' body was, due to the endless number of medications he was taking for various ailments, I told him it was imperative that he drink large quantities of water. This went against his belief, as he was already taking diuretics for his heart. I urged him to drink water in slowly increasing increments, so as not to shock his body, and he chose to comply. This, plus a powerful energetic session, totally released his eczema, much to his joy. The choice was his own, and he moved into total self-empowerment, leading him to experiences beyond those which he had previously limited to medical avenues alone. Charles continued his doctor visits, and his overall health continued to improve.

On the other hand, many people call for assistance and, during their work, find their perfection within, only to resume their daily lives, embracing the old energies they had created, rather than making the changes necessary to commit to the wonderful possibilities open to them. Tanya* was a woman who was aware of great possibilities in her life. A devoted wife and mother, she also knew that her spiritual seeking made her family uncomfortable. As a result, Tanya put herSelf at the bottom of her list of priorities. She kept choosing to squelch her natural gifts, so much so that her body and her emotional state began to rebel.

Tanya was a flower that never fully opened. She always chose to stifle her expansion, using her family and friends as her excuse. She also diminished herSelf by judging others as more "connected" than she was. The result created turmoil within. Tanya had difficulty feeling joy, since she was choosing a joyless path. She went from healer to healer, spiritual guide to spiritual guide, never pausing long enough to allow her own innate connection to bring her to her inner truth. Tanya felt fear that she was missing out, but chose to *keep* missing out by not honoring herSelf. This could change in a moment, once Tanya chooses to embrace her personal magnificence as God.

We choose each moment of our lives. With our choices, we create each experience we live through. We reflect within and without all that we have created through choice. Our choices reflect opportunities to experience Self as God. When you accept your perfection, acknowledge your magnificence, honor yourSelf and choose in selfLove, then you will experience all that you already are.

—BEING—

Being is the experience of living each moment fully, as though it were our first and our last. We choose to experience the exquisite sensation of harmony with whatever is at hand. There is no need to explore the moment to come, nor to hold on to the moment that has passed. Each moment is to be celebrated, each offering an opportunity to discover what we have called forth so that we may learn. Each moment is equal, to be experienced without judgment. There are no "good" moments or "bad" moments; there are only opportunities we have called forth to permit us to explore life fully.

Being is living in grace, which is the experience of Self as pure creation. *Being* recognizes the perfection of ourSelves as creation, and then actively experiences that magnificent creation in all moments. Even when experiencing illness, we can make new choices in selfLove, allowing the illness the opportunity to be released, for the perfection honors body, mind and spirit. As we take full responsibility for every aspect of our lives, we can then take responsibility for bringing ourSelves back to the state of balance within which illness need not exist.

One of my favorite stories is about a young woman who had struggled with dis-ease and physical ailments for many years, as the result of a freak accident which left her totally incapacitated for a full year of her life. The accident had been so severe that doctors were amazed that she survived, and again that she had been able to rebuild her life to its present point.

Marla* was an extraordinary person. Choosing to work as a healer herSelf, she understood everything about diet, exercise, and even about choice. She accepted the limited lifestyle resulting from the accident as something she was creating for herSelf, and that was how she was guided to work with me and my partner, Chris. It took many sessions and much energy to bring Marla to her current experience of powerful healing, but she wanted to work through her blocks and was committed to doing everything required in order to be free, once and for all, from the physical limitations and pain that still plagued her.

Marla chose total self-acceptance; she acknowledged her role in the creation of her physical situation, laying blame on no one, simply understanding that there was a purpose for this creation. She honored Self by choosing holistic healing for her body, mind and spirit. She chose to be pro-active, by tuning in to every detail of her self-created paradigms. And finally, in her love of Self, she, as God, chose to release limitation and embrace her power and her total selfLove. Marla worked hard and gained powerful knowing about herSelf, finding inner peace as a result of her work. As a healer, she then began to expand, for she had greater understanding and was able to communicate more powerfully with her own clients.

We can fully experience the magnificence of *Being* when we totally accept ourSelves as we are. We release all judgment, of Self and All. We look upon ourSelves with the eyes of God and see nothing but the perfection of our own creation. And we know, in all moments, that our life experience is that which we create, as God.

CHAPTER SIXTEEN

The Understanding—Healing Through Love

Health and well-being is experienced through choice.

The magnificence and perfection of each of us simply is. We do not have to become monks in order to lead spiritual, healthy lives. We do not have to be vegetarians, or wear flowing robes, or sit in meditation for hours each day. There is no spiritual "path," because everything is spiritual and all choices are equal. We can work and be parents, husbands, wives, daughters, sons, brothers and sisters, honoring Self and others in each moment. No one is greater than another, for we are all the same. We are here because we chose to experience Self as God. And we all are God.

What we should always honor is our responsibility to Self. We can choose to experience each day in peace, in order to communicate with the silence within. We can choose to honor the physical and never harbor it any ill-will. We can choose to perceive ourSelves as perfect, just as we can choose to see perfection in all things and all people.

Imagine how wonderful it would be if we could visit medical professionals and, rather than asking, "What is wrong?" they would ask instead, "What is your experience?" This simple dialogue would enable us to maintain personal power, rather than diminish our role as a partner and healer. It would also remove judgment, for illness is not "wrong"; it is simply a creation through choice. As we embrace responsibility for Self, we learn to make choices in selfLove.

When we love ourSelves, we cannot fool ourSelves into believing we are what we are not. Many people perceive their realities so differently from their truth. When asked, many clients tell me that they drink *so much* water each day, and yet, when pushed to count the number, some barely get to four glasses per day. Many people purchase nutritional supplements and forget to take them; many eat unhealthful foods, thinking they are fooling someone outside of themSelves; and many are in denial of their emotional make-up, refusing to see their reactions to others as the truth of who they are.

As we acknowledge that we are God, we then embrace responsibility for each moment of our lives. We have always created our lives, but when we understand and accept our power, we begin to choose to live in joy...and love.

Health and well-being is experienced through choice. We should never take a moment of our lives for granted; nor should we take *anything* for granted, for that matter. We can always choose to make the time to honor the people in our lives, as well as the environment we have chosen. Most importantly, we should honor the magnificence of Self.

If you are suffering from any ailment in this moment, know in your heart that it exists as your Teacher. You are the Student. You can choose to learn from your creation of illness by looking into your heart. Discern your choices of selfLove prior to this moment. *Accept* the responsibility for this perfect creation. *Acknowledge* your experience as it is. *Honor* yourSelf from this moment forth, on all levels of mind, body and spirit. *Choose* to live fully and powerfully. And celebrate *being* you!

When experiencing love, you recognize the perfection of Self and the perfection of All. We can all choose to learn to release judgment of everyone and everything around us. Why is it that, when we look upon a tree with damaged branches, we accept the tree as it is with its perceived imperfection, yet, in many instances, when we look upon another person we judge as imperfect, we turn away? As you come into the acceptance of your own perfection, you cannot help but see perfection in all things.

Self-empowerment offers you all the tools you need to create wellness in your body. There is no one outside yourSelf who can heal you, although many can help you release the physical symptoms of your creation. It is important to recognize that, as creator of your illness, you are equally the healer of your illness. The root cause should be addressed, and it is important to face your choices of self-diminishment and to release them once and for all, in order to move into the rest of your life in harmony and balance.

Stop looking outside yourSelf for answers. You have all the answers within your heart. We each, as human Beings who have chosen this physical existence, are here with great purpose. Choose to accept yourSelf unconditionally, and then embrace the choices necessary to change your life and the experience of selfLove. Illness is nothing more than an experience of life and living. You have the power to change the choices which brought forth this experience and live in total joy and love.

Learn to flow in joy each moment. Release judgment of Self and others. Appreciate the small wonders of your life. Share good thoughts and release all other thoughts. Honor your body and your soul. Choose activities which bring you joy. Accept and embrace your power and use it purposefully and honorably. Share your love, and love yourSelf. And as this way of choosing to live each moment of your day becomes a pattern for your life, know that you will not only heal yourSelf, but you will heal all others...through love.

With Appreciation

I choose, with much love, to take a moment to honor and thank those who have made the time to assist me during the final process of completing this book...the loving task of editing, challenging and questioning each chosen word and sentence so that I could more powerfully express my knowing on paper.

Thank you, Michele, for taking my words and turning them into a work of art. As our friendship grows, I will be with you in the moment you recognize the richness of your gift and how wonderful an artist you are.

Thank you, Jodi, for always accepting me with love through the years and lifetimes of our shared experiences of growing and changing. You are my firstborn, my friend, and my powerful teacher. You have blossomed into a butterfly, and I watch you soar into your life and your love of Self with a full and joyous heart.

Thank you, Dara, for choosing to share this experience with me and us all. You have chosen me as your mother in this lifetime, and I have chosen you to teach me to sing as you do. We are connected throughout time, and will sing lifetimes of songs together.

Finally, I thank you, Chris, for holding my hand from the moment we met as though we knew each other from birth. You have guided me throughout my healing from the cancer experience as though it was your experience as well. Together we have accepted our magnificence and discovered our Truth.

As God we are one in all ways...and through choice we are one in friendship and love.

And to you, the Reader, I offer my heartfelt thanks as well. You have chosen to journey through the pages of this book and into your own heart. From this moment forth you have the opportunity to understand your Truth...that because you are God, all that is of your life is of your thoughts...your words...your choices. Choose all experiences through joy and love, and allow your heart to guide you to the magnificent experience of being you!

About the Author

Marilyn Innerfeld is co-founder of *The Worldwide Center* located in Evergreen, Colorado. She is a medical intuitive who identifies anomalies in the physical body, identifies the root-causes of the illness, practices many forms of energetic healing, and provides each person with the tools necessary to proactively heal themSelves. She has been working in the spiritual arena for many years, allowing her intuitive gifts to expand into the healing arena in a natural progression. A certified hypnotherapist, Marilyn Innerfeld is a long-time member of the International Association of Counselors and Therapists. Marilyn has studied nutritional therapies as well as Chinese medicine. She has a mastery of past-life regression in her work as a hypnotherapist, but is currently focused on total wellness through the elimination of present-life issues and blocks. Marilyn has healed from cancer and uses her personal experience to assist her in her work. She works with her business partner Christine Lenick at *The Worldwide Center.*

Marilyn can be reached at center@expandedliving.net.

About The Worldwide Center

The Worldwide Center is an international, personal and spiritual growth teaching center based in Evergreen, Colorado. The cornerstone of The Center's work is the Expanded Living program. The Expanded Living program is offered as self-empowerment workshops, one-on-one teaching sessions, teleclasses and meditation groups that share an expanded life vision, powerful self-help tools and alternative healing techniques. The Center's teaching is based on empowering those who seek to live an expanded life - one filled with joy, deep connection and great fulfillment - with practical tools to free their hearts and heal their bodies.

The Center's vision is to call forth world peace by teaching the power of selfLove. The Center was co-founded in 1999 by Marilyn Innerfeld and Christine Lenick.

Other books published by Healing Arts Publishing include <u>The Simple Truth About God</u> by Christine Lenick.

To contact the Center:

The Worldwide Center

P.O. Box 4223

Evergreen, CO 80437

303-674-7704

www.expandedliving.net

Thank You

As a Special Thanks to the Reader

Begin to live an expanded life today! Visit us at www.expandedliving.net and take advantage of one of our offers as a special way to says thanks for sharing these teachings with us.

—Free *Healing Through Love* On-line Lessons—

Get three *free* Living in Total Wellness Lessons to begin to live fully today by registering as a reader at www.expandedliving.net. Register in the *Healing Through Love* book area by clicking on the Living in Total Wellness Lessons and you will receive your lessons instantly.

—Expanded Living Program Discounts—

The *Expanded Living* program is grounded in teaching an expanded life vision that each of us is magnificent and perfect—mankind's word for God. Looking at ourselves as magnificent and perfect is the most powerful moment of personal truth because it is a mirror for our choice of how we love ourselves. The Expanded Living program is offered either in workshops, teleclasses or one-on-one teaching sessions.

—Expanded Living Workshops and Teleclasses—

The *Expanded Living* Workshop is offered either live or via teleclass. One participant captured the power of the Center's work when she said, *"This course is amazing! The course content is truly revolutionary and will change people's lives in a significantly positive way."*

Get a special **10% reader's discount** on either a workshop or teleclass when you mention that you read one of the Center's books. This discount applies only if mentioned before the completion of the workshop or class.

—Expanded Wellness or Expanded Life One-on-One Sessions—

Over the telephone, from the comfort of your home, you can work one-on-one in private sessions with Marilyn Innerfeld or Christine Lenick. Using spiritual and medical intuitive gifts, Marilyn Innerfeld and Christine Lenick guide clients to heal their hearts and bodies. One time exploratory sessions are available and can be followed by ongoing one-on-one sessions helping you build a powerful and meaningful life tapestry filled with abundance, love and joy.

Take advantage of a special **10% discount** on your first session with either Marilyn Innerfeld or Christine Lenick when you mention that you read one of the Center's books.

—Expanded Living E-Zine Newsletter—

Stay in touch with the teachings of the Center by subscribing to the monthly *Expanded Living* E-zine at www.expandedliving.net.

Contact the Center Today:

The Worldwide Center

P.O. Box 4223

Evergreen, CO 80437

303-674-7704

www.expandedliving.net

Printed in the United States
18089LVS00007BA/1-78